# *Literature-Based*
# Multicultural Activities
## AN INTEGRATED APPROACH

MARY BETH SPANN

*97-09*

SCHOLASTIC
PROFESSIONAL BOOKS

New York • Toronto • London • Auckland • Sydney

**With thanks,
to my adopted German-Irish-Italian-American family
for encouraging me to celebrate a connection
with the people, the customs, and the culture
of my birthplace, Dublin, Ireland.**

## Acknowledgements

I wish to thank Valerie Williams, first-grade teacher at the E. M. Baker School, Great Neck, New York, and Dr. Alene Smith, Associate Professor, Department of Curriculum and Teaching at Hunter College of the City University of New York, for their thoughtful review of this manuscript, and for their valuable insights, suggestions and reactions regarding the literature selections and multicultural activities included here.

I would like also to thank Terry Cooper, Editor-In-Chief of Scholastic Professional Books, for generously sharing her understanding of how the classroom can begin to foster sensitivity and respect for people of all colors and cultures, and to Helen Moore Sorvillo, Associate Editor, for her editorial feedback and encouragements.

Last, but not least, a technical tribute goes to Will Hanley of Custom Computer Specialists in Hauppauge, New York, for patiently talking me through a panic attack when nearly two-thirds of my computer-recorded manuscript temporarily evaporated into the clutches of the "Faulty Disk Demons." Without Will's computer expertise, this book would still be a disk dream.

Designed by Nancy Metcalf
Production and photography by Intergraphics
Cover design by Vincent Ceci
Cover illustration by Jeffrey Weiner
Illustrations by Joe and Terri Chicko

# CONTENTS

*continued*

# Introduction

Good teachers have always tried to respect the belief structures of their students and allow for differences among them, but never before have so many teachers actually taken the time formally to focus curriculum and student attention on cultural diversity and ethnicity, or to infuse these issues into classroom practices each day.

To be fair, until recently, there were very few materials and even less in the way of teacher training to help teachers bring multicultural education to their students. But today, things are finally starting to change.

For this book, we worked hard to gather a list of the best multicultural children's literature available to date, and to create corresponding book-based activities designed to help introduce and develop a classroom awareness of multicultural issues.

Because most of the activities focus directly on helping children discover yet another piece of understanding necessary for a positive multicultural mindset, most of the activities require some teacher direction. They are not necessarily the type of independent activities you can stick in a learning center and expect children to explore on their own. Helping children learn to respect and acknowledge the similarities and differences of the peoples of the world cannot be boiled down to a series of cute activities, nor is it something students learn in isolation.

Multicultural education is an important mission requiring children to exchange ideas and learn new knowledge from outside resources, and from each other. Clearly, a sensitive, informed teacher, acting as guide and facilitator, is the first essential element for growth and success.

Happily, the dawn of literature-based learning provides a new, energized resource for teachers attempting to include multicultural studies in their curriculum. Every day, more and more children's books with a multicultural theme or storyline are being developed and published. Some of these are nonfiction books which offer the reader a peek at a culture and lifestyle which may be quite different, and yet similar, to his or her own. Other books bring legends and folktales to life, offering youngsters storytelling experiences filled with regional twists and overtones. Still other works of fiction bring a rainbow of characters to life, providing authors and illustrators opportunities to share customs and cultures from around the world.

This book is meant to help you introduce multicultural education in your early elementary classroom. The book list suggests grade levels, but feel free to experiment—sometimes a simple book with few (if any) lines of text contains complex themes or concepts suitable for older children, while a longer storybook may be shared, over a few sittings, with younger students. The suggested questions that accompany each book selection are not meant to be staid scripts, but rather are meant to trigger themes and avenues of exploration. Before even reading a particular book selection, you may scan the questions and the activities to see if the book and its related themes interest you enough to give the book a try.

The suggested activities are open to your modifications. For example, if you feel a particular reproducible activity is better used as a discussion springboard than as a writing exercise, trust your instincts. Some of the activities are easier (and require less commitment of time) than others, but they all may be adapted to suit your needs and the needs of your students.

Our hope is that eventually, the concept of multicultural education will be second nature to us all. In the meantime, learning effective ways to welcome the world into your classroom will help insure that you and your students will readily acknowledge, respect and appreciate the differences and similarities that exist among the people of the world.

# Creating a Multicultural Climate in the Classroom

For multicultural education to be effective, it must not be relegated to a special day, week or month on the school calendar. Rather, the study of people and their cultures must be infused throughout the school year, and, depending on your current curriculum and teaching style, this may require modifications in classroom planning and in teaching attitudes and strategies.

Before addressing multiculturalism you may find yourself asking: What *is* a culture? To help you move in the right direction, here are four recommendations to move you and your curriculum through a multicultural makeover:

## ✔ Develop Attitudes That Promote Multicultural Teaching and Learning

For multicultural education to have any impact at all, educators must first recognize and believe in the importance of promoting such learning. When children of diverse backgrounds are taught to acknowledge their differences, they will better be able to discover and embrace the common ground they share. Teachers need to take steps toward a multicultural awareness that demonstrates sensitivity to diversity and support for children who are different—even when those children appear to live outside of the immediate classroom or community.

## ✔ Recognize That Opportunities to Teach Multiculturally Exist in All Areas of the Curriculum

Multicultural awareness may be taught through all areas of the curriculum including language arts, math, social studies, geography and science—you just need to recognize a teachable multicultural moment when you encounter one. When a book features an unusual way of counting or recording mathematical information (as *Eyes of the Dragon* by Margaret Leaf does when it features the abacus), it offers a students a chance to learn about math with a multicultural twist. When a book such as *Where the Forest Meets the Sea* by Jeannie Baker introduces students to an Australian rainforest and coral reef, it offers students a chance to develop a science unit centering on an ecosystem which exists in a faraway land. When it comes to cross-cultural multicultural studies, there's actually a world of possibilities out there!

## ✔ Prepare the Physical Environment to Reflect and Promote Multicultural Learning

A rolled-up map won't teach children much about their world. To send a clear message that multicultural education counts in your classroom, it's important to continually surround students with pictures, posters, maps, globes, and displays reflecting a variety of people, places, customs and cultures. Consider commissioning an artist to paint a world map on your playground or school wall. Set aside at least one of your bulletin boards as a permanent interactive multicultural display (this book will offer lots of ideas to get you started), and set up a multicultural learning center consisting of books, pictures, related activities, student creations and artifacts (on loan from students, teachers and parents).

## ✔ Tap into Multicultural Resources

Literature is a wonderful springboard for introducing multicultural education to your class, but books are only a beginning. When you order classroom supplies, be mindful of your multicultural goals and you'll find that there are many new and exciting products to support your efforts. School supply houses now feature multicultural dolls, puppets, puzzles and crafts, as well as tablets of paper and paints and crayons available in an array of true-to-life skin tones.

Finally, two outstanding must-have resources should be part of any educator's professional multicultural library:

○ *Multicultural Teaching* by Pamela Tiedt and Iris M. Tiedt (Allyn and Bacon, 1990). This book offers teachers cross-curricular multicultural activities. It is a perfect resource for teachers just venturing into the multicultural arena.

○ *Planning and Organizing for Multicultural Instruction* (Addison-Wesley, 1983). This text familiarizes the reader with a history of the multicultural education movement. The book sets forth clear classroom objectives and cross-curricular activities. It also acquaints teachers with additional multicultural resources they will find helpful.

*A note about the listing of the books—with the exception of the first, which relates to all people, they are listed alphabetically, with the country of origin determining the order. If a story is connected to two countries, both are listed (e.g., American and Russian). Hyphenated American titles are listed alphabetically towards the end of the book, with the non-American country determining the order (e.g., Korean-American before Vietnamese-American).*

# Literature-Based
# Multicultural Activities

## AN INTEGRATED APPROACH

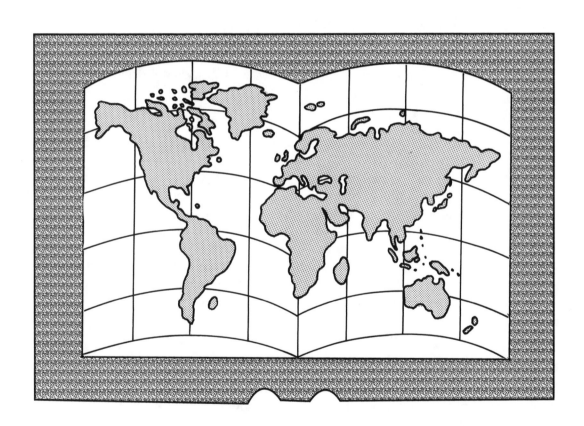

# People

by Peter Spiers
(Doubleday & Co., Inc. 1980. 38 pp.)

*People is a celebration of humanity's similarities and differences. It is the perfect springboard to multicultural awareness in the classroom.*

## Before Reading *People*

○ Have children look closely at the detailed illustration on the cover of *People*. Ask the children to describe as much as they can about the details of the illustration, including the similarities and differences among the people pictured. Ask the children if they think this one book could be about all the people pictured on the cover.

## After Reading *People*

○ Working in an open area, have children group themselves according to physical attributes of eye color, hair color, hair texture and height. Try having the children group themselves according to other criteria such as clothing colors or preferences in food or sports. Aim for some categories which will result in split groupings (e.g., "Everyone who loves to eat olives stand here"), and others which will unite the group in total agreement (e.g., "Everyone who loves to have a day off from school stand here "). Use the exercise to help children understand that each of us shares similarities as well as differences.
○ Call the children's attention to the illustration at the book's conclusion that depicts how the world would look if everybody would "look, think, eat, dress and act the same." Have the children write journal entries about how it would feel to live in such a world.

## FOLLOW-UP ACTIVITIES

### Crowd Scene

Invite children to examine the "crowd scene" on the cover of *People*. Have children work to create a crowd scene bulletin board showcasing all the people they know. Begin by having the children draw themselves (approx. 10″ high) along the lower border of a bulletin board backing paper. Then, have children add other people they know personally to the drawing. Children should begin placing extra people directly behind their own self-portraits, and then work back from there. If possible, have children label each drawing with the person's name and ethnic group. Invite students to continue fitting people into the crowd scene as they occur to the children. Near the board, post a large piece of chart pad paper displaying a running list of the people's names and corresponding ethnic groups represented by your illustrations.

### Partner Discoveries

Help students appreciate similarities and differences that exist between them. Provide students with copies of the activity on page 11. Invite students to work in pairs, completing the page with information about each other. Students should begin by placing their partner's name in the space provided at the top of the form, and then work independently to list the similarities and differences between the two of them. Encourage students to compare and synthesize their lists into one collaborative version, making the final lists as complete as possible.

# People

| | Name | Partner's Name |
|---|---|---|

| Criteria | How We Are Similar | How We Are Different |
|---|---|---|
| Appearance | | |
| Personality | | |
| Activities We Like | | |
| Things We Do Well | | |

# Galimoto

by Karen Lynn Williams
(Lothrop, Lee & Shepard, 1990. 28 pp.)

*When Kondi tells his older brother, Ufulu, that he is going to make a galimoto, Ufulu laughs at him and says that it's impossible for a seven year-old boy to make such a toy. But, with determination and perseverance, Kondi is able to make his dream come true. This story will especially intrigue children who are accustomed to choosing playthings off the toy store shelf.*

## Before Reading *Galimoto*

❍ Use the explanatory notes in the front of *Galimoto* to help familiarize the class with the meaning of the term "galimoto" (a type of push toy made by children from wires or sticks, cornstalks and pieces of yams). Ask if any of the children ever made a toy to play with. Tell them that the story they are about to hear is about a boy who tries to make his own toy, despite some difficulties.

## After Reading *Galimoto*

❍ Ask the children to relate what obstacles Kondi had to face in trying to make a galimoto (e.g., his brother laughed at him, he had trouble getting enough wire, etc.). Have the children describe the positive qualities Kondi demonstrated that helped him see his galimoto project through to completion (e.g., he was patient, he didn't give up, etc.).

FOLLOW-UP ACTIVITIES

## Pinpoint Time

Because *Galimoto* is set in an African village, students may at first think that the story takes place long ago. Ask the children to look closely at the book's illustrations to uncover clues (e.g., contemporary dress, pieces of machinery and tires, galimoto "vehicles," etc.) which help reveal that the story takes place in relatively modern times. Have the children locate parts of the illustrations that might make a reader unfamiliar with life in an African village believe the story happened long ago (e.g., houses with straw roofs, women carrying wares on their heads, etc.). When reading other books in the future, have children rely on story and illustration cues to try and pinpoint the time the stories take place. Keep a running record of your findings. Are there ever stories that are difficult to slot into a particular time frame?

## Invite Playful Ingenuity

By fashioning a toy out of discarded wire, Kondi demonstrates that he is a resourceful boy with creative vision. To foster such resourcefulness in students, bring to class an assortment of "beautiful junk" (e.g., empty egg cartons, old costume jewelery, empty paper towel holders, empty shoe boxes, large plastic caps from liquid detergent bottles, discarded socks, etc.). Place the collection in a large box and invite the students to donate more items to the box. When you are ready to play, have one child reach into the box and pull any object out. Pass the object around the room, inviting children to suggest possible ways to play with each object. Then, fasten each object in the center of a large piece of oaktag or posterboard. Have students work together to illustrate the playful possibilities of each item as shown in the diagram. Display posters in the school hallway. Label display with a large heading reading, "Before you throw it away . . . PLAY!"

## One Special Toy

Provide students with copies of activity page 14. As an introduction to the activity, invite children to imagine that, like Kondi, they have very few playthings. Challenge students to choose which one toy they would wish to own if they could own only that one plaything. In the space provided, have each student draw their special plaything, and on the lines below, have them describe the toy and why it would be the one they would want. (Students may illustrate and write about a toy they already own or one they wish they could own. They may also choose to invent a new toy to play with.)

After the children have completed the exercise and have had an opportunity to share their ideas, ask them to talk about how their lives would be different if their number of playthings was so limited. Would they really miss their toys? What would they do with their free time if they only had one toy?

Name _____

# One Special Toy

_____
_____
_____
_____
_____
_____
_____
_____

# African

# Tower to Heaven

Retold by Ruby Dee
(Henry Holt, 1991. 32 pp.)

*When the sky god, Onyankopon, disappears into the heavens, a wise old woman named Yaa decides that she and the people of her village must work together to build a tower that will allow them to climb up to heaven. They begin building the tower of mortars, but just as the tower nears completion, the people find that they are one mortar short of reaching the heavens. So, Yaa suggests that they take one mortar from the bottom to add to the top, thus creating a story without end.*

## Before Reading *Tower to Heaven*

❍ Show the children the cover of the book which depicts African-looking people walking with objects balanced on their heads. Ask the class to guess which region or country this story has its roots in, then have them explain their hypotheses. Locate West Ghana on a map of Africa. Tell the children that the story told in *Tower to Heaven* has its roots in West Ghana, but that versions of the same story can be found in most of the regions of Africa. (Students may realize that there can be many versions of the same story. In fact, several of the stories in this book, like *Lon Po Po* and *Anancy and Mr. Dry-Bone*, are very similar to stories your students are likely to be familiar with, namely *Red Riding Hood* and *The Golden Goose*. This can be another way of pointing out the similarities among peoples of different cultures.)

## After Reading *Tower to Heaven*

❍ Ask the children to tell if they think the tale told in *Tower to Heaven* could be true or not. Do some parts sound more realistic than others? (If so, which parts?) Have the children discuss reasons why versions of this tale can be found in various African regions (e.g., various regions in Africa have sky gods; people all over the world wish they could converse with higher powers, so the story deals with a popular theme; many stories passed by word of mouth result in different versions of the same story, etc.).

## FOLLOW-UP ACTIVITIES

## Act It Out

Have the children act out the story of *Tower to Heaven*. Have children bring in large plastic mixing bowls to serve as stacking mortars. Drape colorful sheets around students to represent native costumes depicted in the illustrations. Have students decide on a "throne" for the sky god, Onyankopon, to sit upon. (Any elevated spot will do.) Have Onyankopon carry a fan for moving air to create breezes. Provide Yaa with a mortar and pestle. (If you are unable to provide the real thing, a bowl and a wooden spoon or spatula are fine substitutes.)

Read the story for the class to act out. Encourage creative ways to depict scenes impossible to act out literally (such as when Yaa balances atop the tower of mortars.) Older students may enjoy rewriting the tale as a play with narration and dialogue, thus providing scripts for the class. (Be sure to provide choral reading parts so the whole group may participate, and encourage students to take turns playing the parts of Onyankopon and Yaa.)

## Balancing Act

Have the children discover how easy or difficult it is to walk with vessels balanced on their heads. Provide baskets or plastic bowls to serve as vessels. After placing a vessel on his or her head, see how far each child can travel across the classroom. If this method of carrying food or water is so difficult, ask the children to guess why so many people in other countries and cultures make a practice of carrying things on their heads. (If possible, verify their hypotheses with findings from an encyclopedia.) Keep track of how many books read in class depict people from other cultures engaging in this practice.

## Onyankopon's Point of View

In the tale of *Tower to Heaven,* Yaa is a "mouthpiece" for the village, speaking to the sky god on behalf of the villagers. But Yaa's mannerisms and her obnoxious behavior drive the sky god away. Have the children imagine how the sky god feels about being forced to live up in the heavens because he needs to escape from Yaa. Then offer each student a copy of activity page 17 and have them use the page to compose a letter from the sky god, Onyankopon, to Yaa. In the letter, suggest that students offer the sky god's point of view on the whole dilemma, as well as some conditions under which he will return.

Name ______________________________

# Tower to Heaven

______________________
Date

**Dear Yaa,**

Sincerely,
Onyankopon
the Sky God

# African and Jamaican

# Anancy and Mr. Dry-Bone

by Fiona French
(Little Brown and Co. 1991. 26 pp.)

*Rich Mr. Dry-Bone and poor Anancy both want to marry the very clever and very beautiful Miss Louise. Miss Louise decides that she will marry the man who is able to make her laugh. Mr. Dry-Bone tries hard with conjuring tricks, but it is poor Anancy (who must borrow courting clothes from his animal friends) who finally makes Miss Louise burst out laughing.*

## Before Reading *Anancy and Mr. Dry-Bone*

○ Show the children the strikingly beautiful illustrations in the book. Ask the children to describe what it is about the art work (bold, black silhouettes against dazzlingly brilliant Carribean-inspired backgrounds), that makes us want to read the book. If possible, compare these illustrations with the art deco-inspired illustrations found in *Ben's Trumpet* by Rachael Isadora (Greenwillow Books, 1979).

## After Reading *Anancy and Mr. Dry-Bone*

○ Locate Africa and Jamaica on a map. Note that Jamaica is an island in the Caribbean. Inform the children that *Anancy and Mr. Dry-Bone* is only one of many Anancy stories that can be found in both places. Explain that sometimes similar stories develop in cultures that could not possibly have communicated with each other to share stories. In this case, however, natives taken from Africa and enslaved in the Caribbean took their stories with them, so people in both places now tell Anancy stories.

FOLLOW-UP ACTIVITIES

## Similar Stories

As does *Tower to Heaven,* this story demonstrates how different cultures often tell stories with the same concept, conflict or storyline. Tell the children the story of the "Golden Goose" from *The Complete Grimm's Fairy Tales* (Random House, 1972). In this story, which originates in Germany, a princess who never laughs has a father who decides she will marry the man who can make her laugh. How is this story the same or different from *Anancy and Mr. Dry-Bone?* Ask the children to speculate on why similar stories might spring up in very distant cultures.

## Act It Out

Place clothing in the drama trunk so children may act out *Anancy and Mr. Dry-Bone.* Ask children for donations which can be returned to the owners, if desired. Some ideas may include a skeleton Halloween costume, a party skirt or dress for Miss Louise and a "fun-fur" jacket for Anancy. You may also rewrite *Anancy and Mr. Dry-Bone* as a play. Use a large chart pad to help record simple dialogue and setting descriptions. Divide the play into three acts. Act one can use soliloquies to introduce the characters, act two can center on Mr. Dry-Bone's visit to Miss Louise, and act three can depict Anancy borrowing his courting clothes and making Miss Louise laugh.

## Sweetheart Stories

*Anancy and Mr. Dry-Bone* is really the story of how two people fall in love. Have students interview their parents or other relatives or adult friends to discover how the two interviewees met and fell in love. Students should rely on the five W's (Who, What, When, Where and Why) to get as much specific information as they can. Students may discover that parents from different cultures may have had "arranged" matches, or they may have had to obtain their own parents' approval before the marriage could take place. If so, class discussion can focus on the pros and cons of such customs in comparison with the relative freedom Americans expect in choosing a marriage partner. Provide students with copies of the activity on page 20. Have students use the page to record the love story. Students may use space at the top to draw a portrait of the sweethearts interviewed, or the space may be used to display an actual photo of the loving couple. Allow students time to share their interview results.

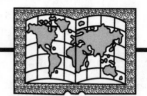

# Anancy and Mr. Dry Bone

## Sweetheart Story Frame

# Where the Forest Meets the Sea

by Jeannie Baker
(Greenwillow Books, 1987. 28 pp.)

*One read through this extraordinary book and the reader feels as though he or she has indeed visited an exotic Australian rain forest. But the sad message at the book's end is that the Australian rain forest, like other ecosystems around the world, is in grave danger of being destroyed. And young readers may be surprised to learn that the beautiful rain forest's most dangerous enemy is us.*

## Before Reading *Where the Forest Meets the Sea*

◯ Help the class locate Australia on a map. Ask the children to describe what they imagine a rain forest must look like. Tell them that you are going to share a book which illustrates Australia's rain forest, located on the northeast coast of Australia.

## After Reading *Where the Forest Meets the Sea*

◯ Ask the children if Australia's rain forest looks like a place they'd like to visit. Show the children where the Great Barrier Reef lies in relationship to Australia and the rain forest. Read about the reef in an encyclopedia to find out why it is so important to Australia's ecology.

FOLLOW-UP ACTIVITIES

## Learning Australian Lingo

Have children scan the book to locate and list unfamiliar words (e.g., reef, cockatoo, creepers, aboriginal). Tell children that good readers often take guesses at the meanings of unfamiliar words. Encourage the children to guess at the meaning of each word they listed and to share reasonings for their guesses. Point out that readers often use context cues (other words and illustrations) to lend meaning to the unfamiliar words. Then, have the children look the words up in the dictionary to see if they guessed correctly.

## Relief Collages

Share with the class the notes following the story which describe how the author/illustrator developed the relief collages she uses to illustrate the text. Then, take a closer look at each lush and detailed illustration. Can the children identify the materials the artist used? Can they find the hidden and transparent pictures present in most of the settings? Ask children why they think the "hidden" pictures were included by the artist/illustrator. (Possibly they suggest animals and people who have inhabited the rain forest.) After examining the illustrations, provide students with pieces of cardboard or oaktag, clay, natural moss (available in plant and craft stores) and glue. Then, take a nature walk and allow children to collect additional natural materials (e.g., leaves, bark, shells, dirt, sand, grass, etc.). Back in class, have children glue the natural materials on the cardboard to create relief collages. Then, have the children draw full-body portraits of themselves on construction paper. Cut and glue fabric bits to the paper dolls to represent clothes. Use markers to add details. Glue completed dolls to the collage so that some of the natural materials overlap the dolls. Have children describe the natural spot they have replicated to the rest of the class. Display the reliefs for all to enjoy. (*Variation* In lieu of paper dolls, actual likenesses of the children may be trimmed from photographs [brought in with parents' approval] and used in the collage arrangement.)

## Understanding Australia's Eco-Threats

Have the class study the unusual illustration on the last two pages of the story. Have the children describe what they see. The author/illustrator uses these pages to hint at the problems which could threaten the rain forest. Provide each student with a copy of the activity on page 23. Help the children list the problems foreshadowed in the book, and then help them list reasons why these problems threaten to harm or destroy the rain forest. In the third column have children list possible ways the threats can be averted.

Author/Illustrator Jeannie Baker lives in Australia.

Name _____

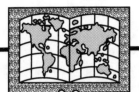

# Where the Forest Meets the Sea

| Problems threatening to Change Australia's Environment | Why Changes Will Hurt Environment | ? |
|---|---|---|
|  |  |  |
|  |  |  |
|  |  |  |
|  |  |  |
|  |  |  |

# Nessa's Fish

by Nancy Luenn
(Atheneum Books, 1990. 29 pp.)

*Nessa and her Grandmother are fishing in the Arctic tundra when Nessa's Grandmother falls ill. How Nessa fends off wild animals while guarding her Grandmother and their catch makes for a satisfying folktale tinged with Arctic lore.*

## Before Reading *Nessa's Fish*

❍ Have children examine the book's illustrations to decide if they have ever been to Nessa's home (or somewhere similar). Ask the children to tell how they know from the pictures whether or not Nessa lives in a city, on a farm, in the suburbs, in the country or elsewhere. (Nessa lives on the coast of Alaska.) Acquaint children with the word "tundra," and look in an atlas to find where the tundra exists. Also, locate Alaska on a map.

## After Reading *Nessa's Fish*

❍ Ask the children to explain why they think the story of *Nessa's Fish* may be true or not. Help the children to understand the difference between fiction and non-fiction books. Acquaint them with the terms and definitions of "legends" and "myths." (The former is a folktale with some truth in it, the latter is a fictitious tale made up to explain a natural phenomenon.) When you read additional book selections, help the children categorize each book accordingly.

### FOLLOW-UP ACTIVITIES

## Ice Fishing

Have children pretend that they live where Nessa lives. Have the children use blocks to form the perimeter of an ice fishing hole. Then, invert a cardboard box and drape with white craft paper (to simulate ice). With a craft knife, cut a hole in the "ice" for the children to fish through. (Important: An adult should do the cutting!) Place paper fish (each fitted with a paper clip) into the hole. Tie a small magnet to the line of a "fishing pole" (consisting of a yardstick or dowel tied to a "fishing line" of string), and allow children to take turns fishing through the ice hole. (Hint: if desired, children may use construction paper and markers to create paper fish resembling those found in Alaskan waters. These fish may be labeled with their correct names and children fishing must identify the fish they have caught.)

## Paper Bag Costumes

Have the children make simple paper bag costumes to use for acting out *Nessa's Fish*. Because the story mentions a "pack of wolves" and "all of the dogs," many children can participate in the retelling. Begin by collecting a supply of brown paper shopping bags. Cut face holes in each as shown in the diagram. Decorate animal bags with markers and paints, and the people's parkas with cotton batting glued around the face opening. Cut up the sides of each bag a bit to allow for arm movement.

## Arctic Investigations

Have children tell about what they believe life in the Arctic must be like. Pass out copies of the exercise on page 26. Have the children fill in the left hand column indicating what they believe various aspects of life in the tundra must be like. Then, read to discover more about the Arctic and the people who live there. Have the class compose a letter to travel agencies requesting travel pamphlets and brochures on Alaska. Record research findings on the right hand column on the activity page. Compare actual findings with the group's speculations. Ask the children to tell whether or not it's OK to prejudge a place without having ever been there.

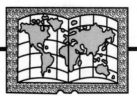

# Nessa's Fish

| | What I Think the Tundra Must Be Like | What the Tundra is Really Like |
|---|---|---|
| Temperature | | |
| School | | |
| Clothing | | |
| Housing | | |
| Jobs | | |
| Transportation | | |
| Recreation | | |

# Very Last Very First Time

by Jan Andrews
(Atheneum, 1986. 32 pp.)

*Eva Padlyat, a small Inuit girl living on Ungava Bay in northern Canada, is getting ready for the first time she will walk on the bottom of the seabed. Eva has walked on the seabed with her mother to collect mussels to eat, but never has she been below the thick sea ice alone. The eerie adventure becomes suspenseful when, beneath the ice, the tide turns and Eva panics. Only when she is safely back with her mother is Eva able to enjoy the idea that this is the last first time she will have to walk on the seabed alone!*

## Before Reading *Very Last Very First Time*

❍ Show the children the book's cover illustration and read the first page of the story to them. Based on what they see and hear, do the children think that the story could be based on fact? Have the children explain their reasoning.

## After Reading *Very Last Very First Time*

❍ Ask the children if they believe now that the story could be based on fact. If they reconsidered, ask the children what helped them to change their minds. Ask the children to take turns explaining why they would or would not enjoy walking on the seabed as Eva does. Why was Eva frightened in the story? Do you think she will ever walk on the bottom of the sea by herself again?

### FOLLOW-UP ACTIVITIES

## Comparing People and Places

Look at the second illustration in the *Very Last Very First Time* which depicts Eva and her mother in their kitchen. Have the children make a list of how the kitchen pictured looks the same as or different from their own. Describe how Eva and her mother look. How do they dress? Look at the third and fourth illustrations which show Eva's neighborhood. Ask: How does it look in comparison to where you live? Use a map to locate Ungava Bay in northern Canada. Have children tell why they think they would or would not like to live in this area.

## Sample Mussels

The mussels that Eva is hunting for are shellfish, often compared to oysters. Visit a seafood store to purchase some fresh mussels for the class to sample (the cooperation of the school's food service staff will be needed for this activity). Send a note home to determine if any students have shellfish allergies before proceeding. After allowing students to handle the mussels, clean the mussels thoroughly to prepare for cooking. (Mussels must be washed in a colander beneath running water and scrubbed with a stiff brush. Clip the fringe material with scissors.) Then, preheat oven to 450 degrees.

Place the cleaned mussels and three tablespoons of olive oil in a large pan. Cook until the shells open. Then, drizzle with melted butter and serve to willing volunteers. After mussels have been consumed, boil the remaining soft matter and fringe material from the shells. Allow students to paint the shells to create jewelry pieces or decorations to hang in a designated "art corner" in the classroom.

## Celebrate Milestones

When Eva emerges from the ice hole, she emerges triumphantly, knowing she finally walked on the seabed alone. Talk with the children about achievements they have accomplished in their lives. (Sometimes achievements are forgotten in pursuit of the next goal, so remind children of achievements they may overlook such as learning to walk, learning to talk, learning how to swing on a swing, slide down a slide or ride a bike, going to school alone, learning how to swim, learning how to read and write, etc.) Provide each child with several copies of the activity sheet on page 29. Cut the sheets apart on the line as indicated. Then, have the children use the spaces provided to illustrate "Things I Am Proud I Have Achieved," and "Things I Want to Do by Myself." Make booklets by stapling each child's activity sheets together between construction paper covers. Have children share their booklets with each other. Point out that while they may not walk on the seabed like Eva did, the children are like Eva because they can celebrate their own personal achievements.

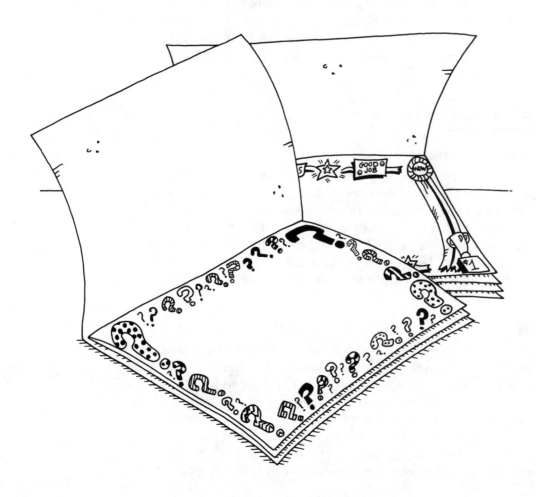

Name _____

# Very Last Very First Time

Things I Am Proud I Have Achieved.

Things I Want to Do by Myself.

# Eyes of the Dragon

by Margaret Leaf
(Lothrop, Lee & Shepard, 1987. 28 pp.)

*To protect the people from wild creatures and evil spirits, a Chinese magistrate surrounds his village with a mighty wall. He then summons a dragon painter to decorate the wall with a portrait of The Dragon King. The finished portrait is magnificent . . . until the magistrate insists that the painter add a dangerous finishing touch: the dragon's eyes.*

## Before Reading *Eyes of the Dragon*

❍ Inform the children that they are going to hear the story of a man who made and then broke a promise. Ask the children if anyone ever made and broke a promise to them. Invite them to share times they broke promises they made to others and then offer opinions about whether it's ever right to break a promise.

## After Reading *Eyes of the Dragon*

❍ Help the children understand that decisions are followed by consequences. What was the consequence of the magistrate's decision to break his promise? How would the story have ended differently if the magistrate had kept his promise? Ask the children to describe why keeping promises might be equally important to people of different cultural backgrounds.

### FOLLOW-UP ACTIVITIES

## Dragon King Paintings

Have the children reread the section in *Eyes of the Dragon* that describes exactly how the dragon painting should appear. Also, share with the class the "Editor's Notes about *Eyes of the Dragon* " (following the book text) which describes the philosophical aspects of a dragon painting. Then, have the children use these directives to create their own dragon paintings. Have the children first sketch their interpretations of how the mural should look, and then, have them team up to synthesize their ideas into final sketches. Provide teams of children with tempera paints and lengths of craft paper. Have the children transfer their sketches to the craft paper, and then use the paints to outline and fill in the paintings. Allow them to decide whether or not they will add eyes to their dragons. Also, allow time for the children to share and explain their artistic interpretations of the dragon. Display paintings together with the heading "Chinese Dragon Kings."

## Get Acquainted with the Abacus

In the *Eyes of the Dragon*, the magistrate uses a Chinese abacus to compute the number of dragon scales the painted dragon needs. Show your class an abacus and, if possible, demonstrate how to use it, or invite another teacher or parent in to present a demonstration. Explain that the abacus is an ancient Chinese counting tool. Ask the children to brainstorm a list of other tools they use for counting (e.g., blocks, plastic counters, Cuisenaire rods, fingers, calculators, etc.). Have samples of counters on hand. Place these items in a designated math corner and allow the children time to experiment freely. Then, have the children make a simplified version of an abacus. Provide them with a supply of plastic beads (available at craft stores), shoe box lids, yarn and craft needles. Knot one end of yarn length and poke through the lid as shown in diagram. Repeat twice more. Then, thread ten beads on each piece of yarn and poke needle through the opposite side of the shoe box lid. Hold the box lid vertically. With a marker, label the bottom row of beads "ones," the middle row of beads "tens" and the top row of beads "hundreds." (To aid in counting, each row of beads may be of a different color.) To have children use their abacus-inspired counting frames, have them first push all beads to the left and push beads to the right as they count.

## Chinese Synonyms

Have children reread *Eyes of the Dragon* and take note of any words they find unfamiliar. Then, provide them each with a copy of page 32 which has space for the children to list these words they find. Have children look the words up in a dictionary and then supply a familiar synonym for each, and list in the appropriate space. Then have children research another culture of their choice to find more synonyms for the Chinese words. Point out that despite different labels that are ascribed to systems and institutions, many cultures share parallel beliefs and experiences.

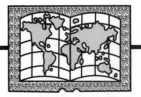

# Eyes of the Dragon

| *Eyes of the Dragon* Vocabulary Words | Meanings | Familiar Synonyms |
|---|---|---|
| | | |
| | | |
| | | |
| | | |
| | | |
| | | |
| | | |

# Grandfather Tang's Story

by Ann Tompert
(Crown Publishers, 1990. 28 pp.)

*In this book, a tangram puzzle becomes a storytelling medium for a little girl and her grandfather. This story-within-a-story text skillfully deals with issues of friendship and pride, while the artwork at once provides the reader with realistic and abstract interpretations of the storyline.*

## Before Reading *Grandfather Tang's Story*

❍ Have the children look at the cover of the book to identify the characters of grandfather and granddaughter. Discuss how the picture of the grandfather looks similar to or different from their own grandfathers. Tell the children that the story is about a grandfather who spends some special time with his granddaughter. Then have the children tell of special times they've spent with grandparents or other older people.

## After Reading *Grandfather Tang's Story*

❍ Help the children understand that stories from a particular country or culture often include animal characters native to the geographical area of the country or culture, and that these animals sometimes take on magical qualities. What animals are included in Grandfather Tang's story? Have the children look these animals up in the encyclopedia to discover if they are native to China. Read aloud the information on fox fairies provided in the back of the book. Ask the children which animals (real or mythical) they would include in a story reflecting the wildlife of their area.

### FOLLOW-UP ACTIVITIES

## Tangram's Origins

Have the children research the origin of ancient tangrams in Chinese folklore. (According to one story, the tangram first came about more than 4000 years ago when a Chinese scholar named Tan was carrying a ceramic tile to the emperor. He accidentally dropped the tile and it broke into seven pieces. In his attempt to repair the tile, Tan discovered the pieces could be used to make other pictures and designs.) Challenge the children to gather and share as much information as possible about the puzzle. If the class's research results in conflicting stories about the origin of the puzzle, ask the children to hypothesize why so many explanations exist.

## Tell Tangram Stories

Have the students take turns working with the puzzle pieces to help tell stories. Begin by retelling *Grandfather Tang's Story*. As you tell the story, arrange the tangram pieces (on a cookie sheet or cutting board) in a shape representing the first character appearing in the storyline. As you continue to recount the story, pass the board to any student. When a second character arrives in the story, have the student rearrange the puzzle pieces to resemble the new character. Continue passing the board to different students until the story ends. Repeat the same story and recruit new student/players.

## Tangram Puzzle Book

Have children do research to find pictures of animals native to China. Provide each of the students with a copy of the tangram puzzle on page 35. Instruct children to carefully cut puzzle pieces apart along all lines and then incorporate all seven pieces into a shape resembling one favorite Chinese animal of their choice. In deciding upon an arrangement, children must be careful not to overlap pieces and should connect each piece to the other pieces along an edge or a point. When children are satisfied with their tangram animals, have them glue arrangements onto contrasting construction paper. Cover each tangram puzzle with a piece of thin copy paper. Show children how to carefully guide pencil along outside of animal shape (not revealing the inside arrangement of the puzzle). Place all of the traced outlines, along with a set of tangram puzzle pieces, together into a "tangram learning center." Children may visit the center and attempt to fit the tangram pieces onto the puzzle outlines created by their classmates. Original tangram animal puzzle pictures may be bound together to form a solution booklet entitled, "Chinese Tangranimals." Place solution booklet into tangram center along with the puzzle outlines.

Swan          Rabbit

# Grandfather Tang's Story

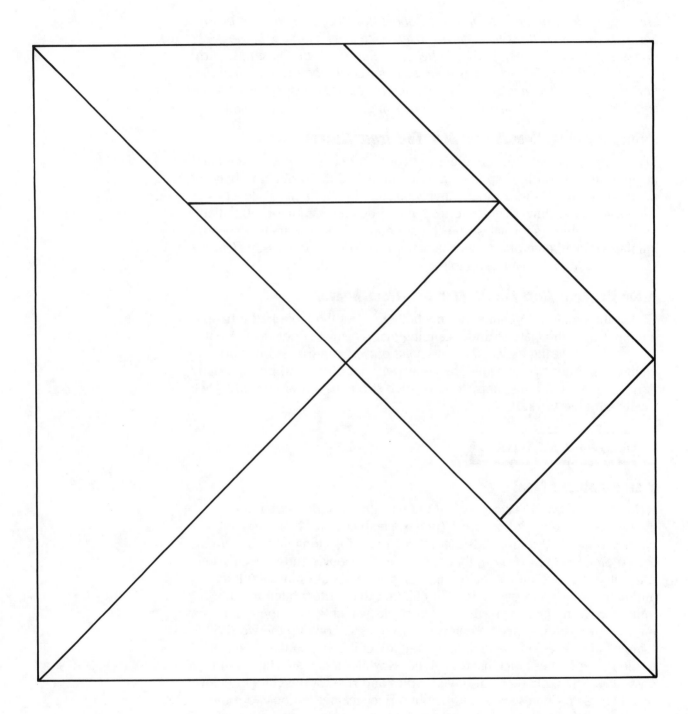

# How the Ox Star Fell from Heaven

retold by Lily Toy Hong
(Albert Whitman, 1991. 28 pp.)

*This is a retelling of the ancient folktale about how the oxen came to be on Earth. According to this Chinese story, oxen once lived in luxury in the heavens with the Emperor of All the Heavens. But, when the most trusted ox messenger, the Ox Star, confuses a message for Earth, the oxen are banished forever from the heavens only to become Earth-bound beasts of burden. What is an unfortunate situation for the oxen becomes a blessing to mankind.*

## Before Reading *How the Ox Star Fell from Heaven*

❍ Tell the class that they are about to hear a story about how an animal came to live on earth. Help the class to understand the distinction between myths (traditional stories usually involving superhuman beings), legends (nonhistorical or unverifiable stories handed down by tradition of earlier times) and fables (short tales to teach a moral or lesson, usually involving animals or inanimate objects as characters). Help them to classify *How the Ox Star Fell from Heaven* as a fable.

## After Reading *How the Ox Star Fell from Heaven*

❍ Ask the children to comment on whether or not the fable had a happy ending. Guide the class to understanding that whether or not story events or endings are pleasing depends on the *point of view* represented by various characters. For example, while the oxen were not pleased to be banished to Earth, the farmers were happy to have such strong beasts of burden to help them with their work.

### FOLLOW-UP ACTIVITIES

### Plan a Chinese Meal

Help children scan the story to find the part that describes what the characters in the book like to eat (rice, vegetables and Chinese sweet cakes). Then, read to the class the notes on Lily Toy Hong, author of *How the Ox Star Fell from Heaven*, that appear on the book's end papers. (Here it is noted that the author "enjoys learning more about Chinese culture and eating rice every day.") Tell the children that writers often include influences from their own lives in their books, which is why the author may have chosen to show people enjoying a rice meal. Look up the words "staple" and "diet" in the dictionary. Tell the children also that rice is a staple in the Chinese diet; have them guess which foods are staples in their own diets. Then, plan a meal of vegetables and rice for the class to enjoy. If possible, use a Chinese wok and bamboo rice steamer to cook your meal, and then consume it using chopsticks, as shown in the diagram on page 37.

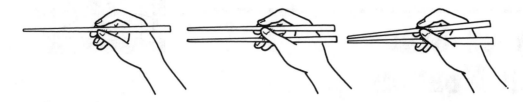

## Compare Stories

Declare one week "Fable Week." In addition to sharing *How the Ox Star Fell from Heaven*, read aloud some of stories in *Just So Stories* by Rudyard Kipling (Weathervane Books, 1978). Included in this collection are fables such as, "How the Whale Got His Throat," "How the Camel Got His Hump" and "How the Leopard Got His Spots."

Tell the class that Kipling's stories were collected from around the world (though they tend to sound alike when told because they are all presented in Kipling's voice). If the children have difficulty understanding Kipling's use of language, feel free to read his words and then translate or clarify what he meant. Encourage the children to illustrate and label or write a brief description of one favorite scene from one of Kipling's tales, or from *How the Ox Star Fell from Heaven*. Also, have them share their illustrations and give examples of how any two stories they listened to are alike or different.

## Conduct TV Interviews

After reading *How the Ox Star Fell from Heaven*, provide students with copies of the character interview sheet on page 38. This sheet provides questions designed to help students discover and appreciate the various points of view the characters held regarding the story's circumstances and outcome. After the children have had a chance to review the questions, encourage them to jot response notes in the space provided. (Younger children may just wish to copy a feeling face to depict how they believe the character felt.) Then, invite students to play the parts of story characters who are guesting on a TV talk show. Play the part of the TV talk show host and introduce your guests, who are seated facing the classroom audience. To interview the characters, use a "microphone" made from an empty paper tissue roll or a cylindrical block. Ask the characters the questions on the sheet, and have the characters respond by referring to their notes and answering. Help your audience note when characters disagree on their point of view. Create new interview questions and repeat the exercise with other stories. (With practice, participants will not need to be familiar with questions ahead of time.)

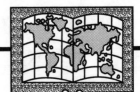

# How the Ox Star Fell from Heaven

 **Interview Questions to Oxen**

1. What was it like to live with the Emperor of All the Heavens in his Imperial Palace?

2. How do you feel about the fact that you got to rest in luxury while people were always tired and hungry?

3. How did you feel when Ox Star confused the Emperor's message? Do you think the punishment was fair? Why or why not? What should have been done instead?

 **Interview Questions to Peasants**

1. How did you feel when Ox Star told his message to you?

2. Describe what life was like without animals to help.

3. Do you think the Emperor's punishment to Ox Star and the other oxen was fair? Why or why not?

 **Interview Questions to Emperor**

1. Why did you allow the oxen to live so easily while people had such a hard life?

2. Do you think your punishment to Ox Star and the other oxen was fair? Why or why not?

3. Do you ever make mistakes?

*Chinese*

# Liang and the Magic Paintbrush

by Demi
(Holt, Rinehart and Winston, 1980. 32pp.)

*Liang, a Chinese boy from long ago, longs to paint, but cannot afford to buy a paintbrush. Then, mysteriously, Liang comes to own a magical paintbrush that brings to life the subject of his paintings! Liang guards the paintbrush's magic until, by accident, the evil emperor learns of the brush's magic and tries to seize it for himself. This old folktale ends on a satisfying note when Liang and his magic paintbrush manage to outsmart the greedy emperor.*

## Before Reading *Liang and the Magic Paintbrush*

❍ Have the class look at the cover of the book. What about the cover suggests that the story comes from China? What about the cover makes us want to read (or reject) the book?

## After Reading *Liang and the Magic Paintbrush*

❍ Ask the children how this story reminds them of another book they have read, namely, *Eyes of the Dragon* by Margaret Leaf (Lothrop, Lee & Shepard, 1987). (If students have not heard this book to date, this is a perfect time to introduce it, as there are many parallels in theme and storyline.)

### FOLLOW-UP ACTIVITIES

## Text and Illustration Cues

What about the book's illustrations suggests this is a story from China? Do the students believe the story takes place in modern times or long ago? How do they know? Have students examine the story text and illustrations to discover which elements seem to be particular to the Chinese culture, and which elements suggest a story of long ago. Do any elements belong in both categories? Record these on the bulletin board or chart pad paper

## Examining and Imitating Chinese Art

*Liang and the Magic Paintbrush* is illustrated with very fine line drawings typical of some forms of Chinese art. Have students notice the fine detail featured in each of the illustrations. In order to provide students with examples of Chinese art work resembling those presented in the book, visit the library to borrow books featuring collections of traditional Chinese art works. Then, provide students with paper and fine line black markers, water-color paints, and (if possible) a supply of Chinese rice paper (available in a variety of grades from art supply stores). Have the children paint illustrations or designs on the paper. (Students may refer to *Liang and the Magic Paintbrush* for illustration inspiration.) When the paintings are dry, have the students outline and detail their drawings with the markers. Display outlined and detailed paintings on a bulletin board titled, "Chinese Rice Paper

Paintings and Drawings." Or, glue paintings to oaktag and fold twice to create mini free-standing folding dividers (as shown in the diagram below) which may be displayed on a table in the classroom.

## "If I Had A Magic Paintbrush . . ."

Liang is lucky enough to own a magic paintbrush, but quickly learns he must act responsibly for what he brings to life. Provide students with copies of activity page 41. Have students use the top half of the page to draw or paint what they would paint if they owned a magic paintbrush. Then, have students use the bottom half of the page to draw or paint what would happen (good or bad) if the subject of the painting came to life. Encourage students to label their illustrations. Students may repeat the activity as often as they like. Staple students' collections together between construction paper covers to create "(Student's name) and the Magic Paintbrush" booklets.

# Liang and the Magic Paintbrush

If I had a magic paintbrush . . .

_____

_____

_____

_____

_____

_____

_____

# Lon Po Po: A Red Riding Hood Tale from China

Translated by Ed Young
(Philomel Books, 1989. 32 pp.)

*The tale of Lon Po Po, the wolf, parallels the European tale of "Little Red Riding Hood." This Chinese version is believed to be more than a thousand years old. As translator and illustrator, Ed Young relied on a combination of ancient Chinese panel art and contemporary pastels and watercolors to create dramatic illustrations that successfully complement a powerful text.*

## Before Reading *Lon Po Po*

○ Ask how many of the children have ever heard the story of "Little Red Riding Hood." Ask the children briefly to recount the familiar tale, then tell the class that they are about to hear a Chinese version of the same tale. Ask the class to imagine how the story might be the same or different from the (European) version that they are probably familiar with.

## After Reading *Lon Po Po*

○ Hold a brief discussion about how the two versions of "Red Riding Hood" were, in fact, the same, and how they differed. Invite students familiar with both versions to tell which version they liked better, and why.

FOLLOW-UP ACTIVITIES

## Exploring Panel Art

Ed Young's illustrations feature contemporary watercolors and pastels on ancient Chinese panel art. Ask the class to comment on the effectiveness of combining these techniques—what feelings do Young's illustrations evoke? On the chalkboard or large chart pad, have children suggest a list of reasons why the illustrations in *Lon Po Po* are especially scary (e.g., part of almost

each illustration is hidden, the illustrator uses lots of dark colors, the eyes in the pictures look frightful or scary, etc.). Suggest that students try their hands at panel art. Have students use watercolors to paint a picture on a large piece of construction paper (or on pieces of Chinese rice paper available in art supply stores). When they dry, cut the pictures into three or four vertical panels of equal size. Mount each panel on a contrasting construction paper mat slightly larger in size than the painted panel. Mount the matted panels on a larger piece of construction paper or craft paper cut to size. Display in a large area (such as a hallway) with a label reading "Chinese Panel Art."

## Appreciating Vocabulary

Reread the book to the class and have students raise their hands when they hear a vocabulary word they don't comprehend and/or a word that is particular to China or the Chinese culture. These may include hemp, gingko, and "Hei yo." Challenge the children to guess at the words' meanings from context cues. Ask the children in class to discuss what words they would substitute for the culturally-inspired words in questions if they were retelling the story, in order to make themselves understood in their own culture. Ask the class to tell why they believe learning such vocabulary may help us to understand and appreciate other people and foreign cultures.

## Story Comparison

To acquaint the entire class with the European version of "Little Red Riding Hood," share a book such as *Little Red Riding Hood* by Trina Schart Hyman (Holiday, 1983). Then, provide each student with a copy of the activity on page 44. Tell students that this activity will help them better see how the two stories are alike and how they differ. Complete the page as a class, or in small groups, encouraging students to share information. Students may jot brief answers in the spaces provided (pre-writers may choose to sketch their responses instead).

Translator/Illustrator Ed Young was born in Tientsin, China and grew up in Shanghai.

# Lon Po Po

| | Lon Po Po | Little Red Riding Hood |
|---|---|---|
| Where we meet the wolf | | |
| What the characters call the Grandmother | | |
| Where the mother is during the wolf's visit with the children | | |
| Who saves the children | | |
| What happens to the wolf | | |
| How the story ends | | |

# Our Home Is the Sea

by Riki Levinson
(E. P. Dutton, 1988. 32 pp.)

*As they follow a boy on his way from school to the houseboat where he lives, young readers are treated to a trip through the busy city streets of Hong Kong. But the boy is not as interested in the city hustle as he is in the sea which surrounds his Hong Kong home. His mother says he will grow up to be a teacher, but in his heart the boy knows that, like his father and grandfather before him, he will grow up to be a fisherman and his home will always be the sea.*

## Before Reading *Our Home Is the Sea*

○ Locate Hong Kong on a map. Point out that Hong Kong is comprised of a tiny island plus some coastland area located on mainland China. Tell the children that people who live so close to the sea have a close relationship with the water (i.e., the sea is an important part of their lives). Tell the children that this is the story of a boy who lives in Hong Kong. Write the new Chinese vocabulary words the children will encounter (appearing on the copyright page, located in the front of the book) on a chalkboard or chart pad. Tell the children to listen for the words, but do not yet disclose their meanings.

## After Reading *Our Home Is the Sea*

○ Review the text to locate the new vocabulary presented in the book. Print the sentences on a chart pad. Cover each new word with an index card. Have children attempt to fill in the blank cards with an English synonym for the concealed Chinese word. This exercise encourages students to guess the words' meanings from context clues alone. Compare their guesses with the definitions presented in the book.

### FOLLOW-UP ACTIVITIES

## Tai Chi Demonstration

Have students look carefully at the illustration which depicts the old man "standing straight and still under a gingko tree." Inform the children that the man pictured is performing *tai chi*, an ancient Chinese form of exercise. To further acqaint the children with tai chi, invite a tai chi instructor to the class to explain the philosophy and demonstrate the technique behind the movements, or borrow a tai chi demonstration video (available from libraries or video rental stores). Allow students the opportunity to practice and demonstrate tai chi movements. How does this form of movement differ from other types of sports and exercise the children are familiar with?

## Sample Congee and Tea

In the story, the boy and his family dine on *congee* and tea. Make congee and tea for your students. According to the glossary (appearing in the front of the book), congee is a thin rice soup.

**Congee Soup**

   ½ cup rice
   4 quarts water
   ¼ pound dried shrimp or scallops (optional)
   dash salt

Place ingredients together in a large pot. Bring to boil and simmer for three hours. Serves 8–10. Serve with Chinese tea, if desired.

## "Hong Kong Or My Home" Card Game

Provide each student with a copy of page 47. Use additional copies of the same page to record these things found in the story: the sea, a tram, market streets, amahs (nurses or maids), birdmen, peacocks, a wharf, a sampan (a very small boat). Add to these items some items found only in the students' neighborhood (e.g., specific shops and businesses, landmarks, etc.), and other items found in both places (e.g., report cards, streets, street lights, apartment buildings, school buses, parks, etc.) After printing all the items in the boxes, glue the pages onto construction paper. Let dry and cut the boxes apart, thus creating playing cards. Place these cards face down on a table. Allow children to take turns choosing a card and placing that card under the column labeled "Found in Hong Kong" or the column labeled "Found in _____ (the children's homeplace)." Items found in both places should be placed in the column labeled "Found in Hong Kong and in _____ (the children's homeplace)." Each student should attempt to be the first to fill his or her entire activity sheet with cards.

Name _____

# Our Home Is the Sea

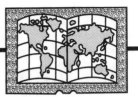

| Found in Hong Kong and in — Student's homeplace | | | | | |
|---|---|---|---|---|---|
| Found in — Student's homeplace | | | | | |
| Found in Hong Kong | | | | | |

# The Day of Ahmed's Secret

by Florence Perry Heide and
Judith Heide Gilliland
(Lothrop, Lee and Shepard, 1990. 32 pp.)

*Ahmed has a secret: He has learned to write his name! But, before young readers learn Ahmed's secret, they are treated to a modern look at the ancient city of Cairo. Throughout the book, the reader's senses are met with an outpouring of the rich sights, sounds and flavors of the Middle East. But, in the end, it is Ahmed's secret that allows readers to understand how much they are like the boy from faraway Cairo.*

## Before Reading *The Day of Ahmed's Secret*

○ Challenge students to locate Cairo, Egypt on a map. Ask what they think of when they think of Egypt—King Tut, camels, the Sahara desert and the Great Sphinx, and pictures discovered inside pyramids of stiff-armed people who seem to be walking sideways may come to mind. Students may be surprised to learn that Egypt has modern cities, too. Tell them that this story is about Ahmed, a boy who lives in Cairo. Spread open the cover of the book in order to display the panoramic illustration of the Cairo marketplace. Ask the children to tell what is familiar and what is unfamiliar about the place as pictured.

## After Reading *The Day of Ahmed's Secret*

○ Ask the children if they would like to trade lives with Ahmed. What parts of Ahmed's life would be fun and interesting? What parts would be difficult? What parts of their lives would be difficult for Ahmed? Fun for Ahmed?

## FOLLOW-UP ACTIVITIES

## Old and New

*The Day of Ahmed's Secret* is set in the ancient city of Cairo. The book's illustrations are full of references to the ancient and modern aspects of this city. Explain to the students that Cairo is much older than any city in America. Have children scan the illustrations to discover elements that seem to suggest that the story takes place long ago. Then, take a second look at the illustrations to discover indications that the story is indeed set in modern times. Have the children speculate as to whether or not Cairo is a city they would like to live in. Ask: How is Ahmed and his lifestyle the same or different from yours? Taking your class on a walking trip may help point out that there are old and new elements in your own neighborhood. If you take along a camera, you may be able to create an "old and new" display.

## Sensory Hunt

In *The Day of Ahmed's Secret*, Ahmed tells of the sounds and colors and flavors of the city of Cairo. Cover a bulletin board with craft paper and create a grid as shown in the diagram. Have children fill in the chart with the sounds, colors and flavors of Cairo as cited in the book. Then, have students pay attention to such sensory stimuli for other settings of their choice, and add information regarding these settings to the chart. Some suggested settings might include their neighborhood, the classroom, the cafeteria, the school bus, etc. If possible, add photographs of the settings to the chart. How do the student's familiar settings compare to Ahmed's city of Cairo?

| Setting | Sights | Sounds |
|---------|--------|--------|
| Cairo | | |
| Cafeteria | | |

## What's In a Name?

Ahmed was so proud when he learned how to write his own name. Help your students celebrate pride in their own names by having them create name collages using the worksheet on page 50. Give each child a copy of the worksheet, some sheets of newspaper, glue and scissors. Have the children (1.) look through the newspapers for the letters that spell their own names, (2.) cut or tear them out, and (3.) glue the individual letters across the top of the empty space on the worksheet, spelling out their names. The rest of the worksheet should be filled with words and pictures cut or torn from the newspaper and glued in place to give an impression of the child's likes, dislikes and personality (e.g., a horoscope for the student's birth date, a picture of a cat for a child who loves animals, cut-out letters that spell out the child's hobbies, like cycling, reading, or swimming, etc.). Display finished "What's In a Name" collages around the room.

# The Day of Ahmed's Secret

## What's In A Name?

Cut letters and pictures from newspapers and magazines and glue in the space below to spell your name and tell all about you—what you like, your pets and hobbies, what you want to be when you grow up, or anything you like.

## French and Italian

# Sing, Pierrot, Sing
by Tomie dePaola
(Harcourt Brace Jovanovich, 1983. 32 pp.)

*This story, fashioned from French pantomime and from the Italian commedia dell'arte, recounts the story of Pierrot, a moonstruck mime who attempts to win the heart of the lovely Columbine. But, sadly for Pierrot, Columbine is already in love with Harlequine and cannot return Pierrot's affections. Without printed word, the author manages to convey the universal pain of unrequited love, and the eternal hope that twinkles beyond the sadness.*

## Before Reading *Sing, Pierrot, Sing*

○ Ask the children if they can demonstrate how it is possible to talk to each other without words. Offer the class concrete suggestions for wordless communications (e.g., "Can you say good-bye with out words?" and "Can you show that you are hungry without words?"). Ask the children if they believe it is possible to tell a whole story without words. After listening to their responses, ask if students have ever seen a mime. Explain that there is a storytelling art form known as *pantomime* that helps the storyteller convey a whole story without words. Then begin "reading" *Sing, Pierrot, Sing*, a wordless picture book about such a pantomime performer.

## After Reading *Sing, Pierrot, Sing*

○ Ask the class to reiterate the range of feelings demonstrated by the character of Pierrot. Ask: Without hearing his words, how are we able to tell what Pierrot is feeling?

### FOLLOW-UP ACTIVITIES

## Appreciating Pantomime

Use information from an encyclopedia to further acqaint the class with France and the ancient French art of pantomime. Also, share a book on mime, such as Mime: Basics for Beginners by Cindie and Matthew Straub (Plays, 1984) which provides a basic introduction to the history and art of pantomime. Be sure to make children aware that pantomime (like the oral tradition of storytelling) is reflected in a variety of cultures including French, Italian and English. Look on a map and have children speculate how these three countries/cultures might come to share an art form. If possible, have a mime perform for your class, or for the whole school. (Contact your local college or university drama department to see if a drama student familiar with pantomime could volunteer to provide a brief demonstration.)

## Mum's the Word

Challenge your class to spend a block of time (such as during recess or during lunch) not speaking or writing words to each other. Tell the children that they are allowed to communicate, but only through pantomime. To close the exercise, have the children write how they felt about the experience.

## Mimic Mime's Movements

Make copies of the movement cards on activity page 53. Use glue to mount the pages on construction paper before cutting the cards apart. Have pairs of children select one card and pantomime the scenario described thereon while the rest of the class tries to guess what they're doing. Remind children that they must "show" the audience any props they expect the audience to "see." (*Hint: If your class has been unable to become an audience to a mime performance, consider demonstrating and having students guess some simple scenarios [e.g., putting on shoes and socks, brushing teeth, opening an umbrella in the wind, etc.] before expecting the children to perform.) After the students have had a chance to perform, have the rest of the class try to guess what the students were acting out. If the pantomime activity is popular with the group, consider having students record their own original scenarios on index cards for classmates to perform.

# Sing, Pierrot, Sing

 Mimic taking a bath.

 Mimic answering the telephone and hearing great news.

 Mimic reading a book that is at first funny, and then sad.

 Mimic making a peanut butter and jelly sandwich.

 Mimic eating a drippy ice cream cone.

 Mimic trying to walk a large dog who is tugging on her leash.

 Mimic trying to drink a very hot cup of cocoa

 Mimic putting on roller skates and trying to skate for the first time.

 Mimic swinging on a swing. Then, mimic sliding down a fast slide.

# Clancy's Coat

by Eve Bunting
(Frederick Warne & Co., 1984. 44 pp.)

*Tailor Tippett and Farmer Clancy are the best of friends. But, when Tippett's cow, Bridget, tramples Clancy's garden, the two friends become enemies, fast. Only when the cold March winds force Clancy to take his overcoat to the tailor for mending does the friendship begin to mend as well.*

## Before Reading *Clancy's Coat*

○ Ask the children if they've ever had an argument or disagreement with a friend. Ask students to tell why it is sometimes easy to get angry and argue and much more difficult to make up. Tell the class that the book you are about to share is about two characters who used to be friends until an argument came between them. Now they are struggling to become friends again.

## After Reading *Clancy's Coat*

○ Have the children explain how each of the men felt when Bridget the cow ruined Clancy's vegetable garden. Does each man believe that he is right? Is it possible that two different points of view could be right at the same time? Discuss.

---

### FOLLOW-UP ACTIVITIES

---

## For Argument's Sake

Clancy and Tippett each thought he was right. Neither could see the other's point of view. Ask students to group themselves into those who think Clancy was right and those who agree with Tippett. After they discuss the merits of their points of view, have them role-play, reversing roles to try to see and express the other viewpoint.

## Irish Tea Party

In *Clancy's Coat*, the two men mend their friendship over tea and bread, and the Irish, like the Russians, Chinese, Scots, and English, are closely associated with tea drinking. Students will enjoy celebrating their friendships with an authentic tea party (ask the cafeteria staff for the use of their oven).

To help with the party planning, send a note home asking to have the children bring in one cup and saucer (or one mug) each, as well as any teapots parents are willing to lend. (Parent involvement in this activity can be encouraged as much as possible.) Visit a health food store to purchase decaffeinated Irish tea bags. Plan to serve tea with cream, sugar and honey. Then, help the children make an Irish soda bread, according to the following recipe, to sample with their tea (children can take turns measuring, mixing, shaping the loaf, and timing the baking, but you or another adult will have to do the cutting with a very sharp bread knife to achieve the thinnest slices):

## Irish Soda Bread

4 cups all-purpose flour (unbleached is best)
2 teaspoons salt
¾ teaspoon baking soda
¾ teaspoon double acting baking powder
1½ to 2 cups buttermilk
⅛ cup caraway seeds and/or ¼ cup dried
currants (optional)

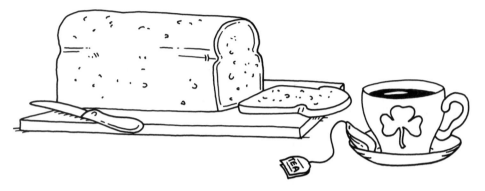

Combine dry ingredients and mix *thoroughly*. Add enough buttermilk to make a soft dough (like biscuit dough) that will hold its shape. Knead on a lightly floured surface for 2 to 3 minutes, until smooth. Form into a round loaf and place on a greased cookie sheet. Cut a cross on top with a sharp knife and bake at 375° for 35 to 40 minutes. (The loaf is done when it sounds hollow when tapped.) Let cool *completely* before slicing *very* thin and serving with butter.

## Irish Stitchery

Because Tippett is a tailor and because the Irish practice fine stitchery in making lace and embroidery, have the children use the pattern on page 56 as a stitch guide to help them try their own hand at stitching. Before working on completing the picture suggested by the stitch guide, provide children with needles, embroidery floss and felt or burlap scraps, so that they may learn and practice the simple stitches suggested on the guide. Then, have the children pin copies of the stitching guide to a separate piece of felt or burlap (9″ × 12″). Show them how to stitch through the paper and the felt. When completed, gently tear the paper away from the stitches and the fabric.

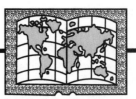

# Clancy's Coat

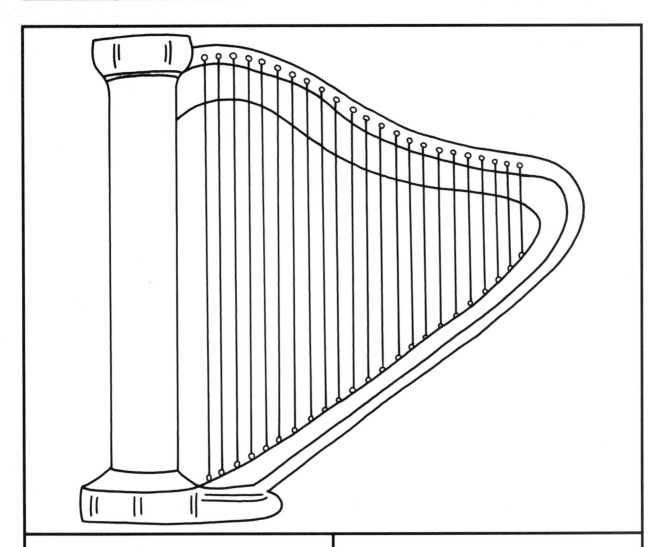

## Stitches to Try:
All stitches begin by drawing needle up through fabric at #1.

### Straight Running Stitch

up at 1   2 3   4 5   6 7   8   9

### Cross Stitch
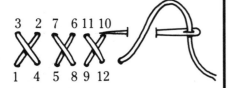
3 2 7 6 11 10

1 4 5 8 9 12

### Blanket Stitch
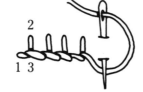
2

1 3

### Satin Stitch

2468

1357

stitches lay very close to each other to fill open space

# Crow Boy

by Taro Yashima
(Viking Press, 1955. 37 pp.)

*Through text and illustrations, this book paints a portrait of a child who learns differently from his classmates, and it also pays tribute to the teacher who understands. By demonstrating the importance of respecting an individual's learning styles and strengths,* Crow Boy *is as much a book for teachers as for children.*

## Before Reading *Crow Boy*

○ Have the children look closely at the illustrations in *Crow Boy*. How do the people and the school look the same as or different from what the children are familiar with? Tell the children that the book is about a boy who looks and lives much like his classmates, but still feels very different. Invite the children to discuss how it is possible to be the same and different from others at the same time. You may want to make a chalkboard chart with headings "How We Are Alike" "How We Are Different" and list the children's answers.

## After Reading *Crow Boy*

○ Even though Chibi did not like school, by the end of sixth grade he was honored for having a perfect attendance record. Have the children talk about what is valued in their school. What honors (if any) are awarded in their classroom or school? Why do the students believe these qualities or behaviors hold value to the teachers and administrators who bestow the awards?

FOLLOW-UP ACTIVITIES

## The Classroom All Around Us

Chibi had difficulty learning in school, but outside of the classroom he learned many things, including how to imitate complicated crow calls. Have children talk about things they learn outside of school. Use a large chart pad to make a running list of "Things We've Learned Outside of School." Ask students if it would be likely that if Chibi went to their school he would have learned to imitate crow calls. What would he have been likely to learn? Help the class to understand that what we learn is influenced by where we live. Ask the children to imagine what they would be likely to learn if they lived in different places (e.g., near a lake, in the desert, in the forest, in an apartment in the city, in the jungle, etc.).

## Writing Styles

*Crow Boy* features illustrations of Chibi's Japanese character handwriting. Ask the children how the Japanese writing looks the same as or different from their own. Collect samples of different alphabets (international food boxes and menus are a good source, or look in the library for illustrated editions of alphabets) and compare the look of each one. Cover a bulletin board with a length of colorful craft paper. Using paint or markers, have the children copy examples of the alphabet characters directly onto the craft paper. Label each sample with the culture of origin. Have the children keep their eyes peeled for additional alphabet samples they may staple directly to the board. (These are sometimes available in merchandise packing material, or can be found in travel brochures.) If possible, have visitors from different cultures explain their systems of written communication.

## Something to Crow About

Talk with the children about how Chibi's differences are at first seen by some as being bad or wrong, and in the end are seen by all as being quite special. Help the class to understand that whether a trait is seen as a shortcoming or a strength is largely a matter of point of view. Provide children with copies of page 59. Brainstorm together to generate more shortcomings to add to the list appearing in the left-hand column. Then, help students "reframe" each shortcoming as a strength as demonstrated in the right-hand column. Ask the children to tell why it's important to focus on such traits found in ourselves and others as strengths, rather than as shortcomings.

*Crow Boy's* Author/Illustrator Taro Yashima is Japanese.

Name _____

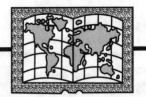

# Crow Boy

*Changing* **Shortcomings** *into* **Strengths**

| | |
|---|---|
| | |

# *Japanese*

# Sachiko Means Happiness

by Kimiko Sakai
(Children's Book Press, 1990. 32 pp.)

*Ever since little Sachiko was born, she had a special relationship with her grandmother, who shares her name. But as Sachiko's grandmother ages, she changes so much that, eventually, she cannot even recognize her own granddaughter. How Sachiko and her family come to accept Grandmother's illness is testimony to the strength of a family's love.*

## Before Reading *Sachiko Means Happiness*

❍ Ask the children to tell what about the book invites us to read the story. Based on these attributes, what do the children believe the mood of the book will be?

## After Reading *Sachiko Means Happiness*

❍ Remind the children of their predictions regarding the mood of the book. Did they guess correctly? Ask the children if they would feel the same or different if they were in Sachiko's place. Is the story one that could only take place in a Japanese family? Why or why not? Encourage children to share their own experiences to support their beliefs.

## FOLLOW-UP ACTIVITIES

## Bittersweet Inspiration

In the book's afterward notes, Kimiko Sakai, author of *Sachiko Means Happiness,* tells of the bittersweet story of her own grandmother in Japan who suffered from Alzheimer's disease. Invite the children to describe times they have had to deal with illness in their own families. Were their feelings the same or different from young Sachiko's in the book? Help the children to understand that some feelings are universal and affect us the same way regardless of culture or ethnic group. Suggest that the children consider writing "bittersweet books" recalling times that are both happy and sad (e.g., the end of the school year, a visit from a friend or relative that must come to an end, outgrowing old toys or clothes, etc.) Also, suggest that children decorate their book illustrations with beautiful "flower boxes" as are featured in the book. Pictures of Japanese flowers can provide inspiration, and you may also show children how to draw the bittersweet vine which may also be used to enhance their writing.

## Name Game

In Japan, "Sachiko" means "happiness." Students may be surprised to discover that their names have special meanings, too. Send a note home asking to borrow "ideas-for-naming-your-baby" books. Such books often include hundreds of names, plus the cultural origins and underlying meanings of each. After collecting the books, look up the children's names and record your findings. Have the children record their names, meanings and origins on copies of the leaf pattern on page 61, which may be colored and used for a bulletin board border. Have children repeat the exercise with the names of family and friends, recording the information on the lines provided, and creating a border leaf for each "extended-family-class" member. How many different cultures are the children able to represent?

Author Kimiko Sakai lives in Tokyo, Japan.

# Sachiko Means Happiness

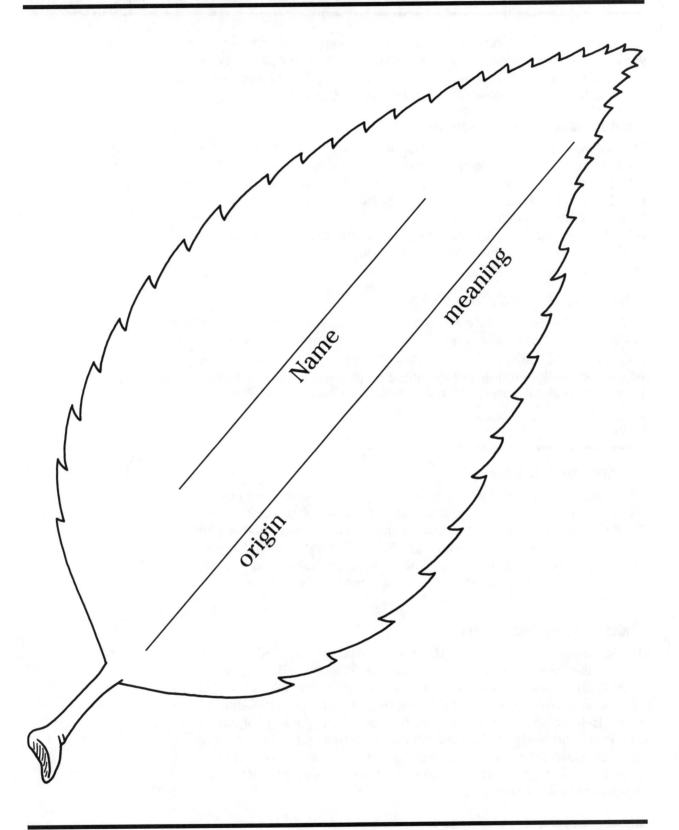

Name

meaning

origin

# The Chinese Mirror

Adapted from a Korean Folktale
by Mirra Ginsburg
(Harcourt Brace Jovanovich, 1988. 26 pp.)

*This humorous Korean folktale tells the story of people who have never seen themselves in a mirror before. The mirror causes nothing but problems—and only when the mirror is destroyed can the people once again focus their attention on each other rather than on their mirror images!*

## Before Reading *The Chinese Mirror*

❍ Pass around a very small mirror and instruct each child to look closely at his or her reflection and describe what he or she sees. As each child looks into the mirror, ask if he or she can see other things, such as the face of a friend or what's happening outside that they can see through the window. Then, have the children stand before a full length or wall-size mirror and describe what they see. Are they able to see more than the reflection of their own faces? The exercise should help the children understand the dilemma faced by the characters in the book.

## After Reading *The Chinese Mirror*

❍ Ask the children to locate Korea on a map. Judging from the illustrations in *The Chinese Mirror*, what kind of land and lifestyle do the children believe they would find in Korea? Help children consult modern day geography books and articles on Korea to see if they were correct in their assumptions. If the story is about Korea, why is the book titled *The Chinese Mirror?*

## FOLLOW-UP ACTIVITIES

## Sharing Point of View

The mirror causes much unhappiness among the characters because it allows each person to see only one narrow perspective or point of view. Have the children talk about times they had trouble seeing another person's point of view (or convincing someone else of their own ideas). Have the class suggest ways to better understand or share points of view. Post these ideas on a large chart pad and refer to them when disagreements arise in the class.

## Understanding Korean Art

The illustrations in *The Chinese Mirror* were inspired by the paintings of two eighteenth-century Korean genre painters, Sin Yun-bok and Kim Hong-do. Consult art books from the library to discover more examples of Korean art. How is modern-day Korean art different from the illustrations featured in the book? Help children brainstorm a list of reasons why the look of one country or culture's art might change through the years (e.g., due to print media, telecommunications and ease in travel, artists today are more easily influenced by art from other cultures; artists today have different tools and equipment to work with; etc.).

## Mirror, Mirror On the Wall

Provide children with copies of the activity on page 64. Work together to generate some initial ideas about what we can and cannot tell about ourselves from looking in the mirror. Record these on a large chart pad. Then, have children work independently to complete their lists; add the children's ideas to the chart pad list to see how many ideas the whole group can generate. Help children use this activity to understand that we are limited in what we can or cannot tell about someone from another ethnic group or culture by appearance alone. Have each child cut out the shape of the mirror and glue it onto stiff construction paper or cardboard. (You may want to provide shiny metallic gift wrap for them to glue to the front for more of a "mirror" effect.) If using metallic paper, have students write their lists of "Things we can tell from looking in a mirror" and "Things we can't tell from looking in a mirror" on plain paper they can then affix to the mirror in two columns, as shown. If not using metallic paper, have the students write directly on the reproducible, as indicated. Display the "mirrors" on a bulletin board entitled "Mirror, Mirror on the Wall."

Mirror, Mirror On the Wall

# The Chinese Mirror

Things we can tell from looking in a mirror

Things we can't tell from looking in a mirror

# Borreguita and the Coyote

Retold by Verna Aardema
(Alfred A Knopf, 1991. 32 pp.)

*When he spots a little lamb known as Borreguita, Coyote thinks he's found a perfect little meal. But, time and again, the little lamb uses her wits to outsmart the Coyote. Not only does she manage to escape a mean fate, but she makes certain that Coyote never bothers her again.*

## Before Reading *Borreguita and the Coyote*

❍ Tell the class that you are about to share a book set in Mexico. Locate Mexico on a map. From the cover, can the children infer anything about the climate or terrain of Mexico? What do they notice about the colors the artist used on the cover? Have children study the cover of the book to see if they can discover any clues telling what the book is about. Record the children's guesses on a chalkboard or on a chart pad.

## After Reading *Borreguita and the Coyote*

❍ Compare the children's storyline predictions with the actual story. Were students able to guess correctly what the story was about? Ask the class if it is always possible to judge a book by its cover. Have the children locate books in your class library that do not have especially revealing covers.

## FOLLOW-UP ACTIVITIES

## Gather Spanish Glossaries

In the front of the book, the author provides a brief glossary and pronunciation guide to some Spanish words used in the story. Print these on the chalkboard or on a large chart pad. Review these with the class and ask the children if any of them can add any additional Spanish words or phrases to the list. Invite a Spanish teacher or Spanish-speaking guest into your class to teach the class additional Spanish words and phrases. Locate Mexico and Spain on a map or globe. Ask your guest to explain why people in Mexico speak Spanish, the native language of Spain. Consider having students copy the Spanish glossary into notebooks, illustrating their entries and leaving room for new additions. (Hint: Place a Spanish-English dictionary in the writing corner and encourage children to add new words to their glossaries.)

## Sample Mexican Food

Here's a simple Mexican meal—Meatless Tacos—which may be prepared, with adult supervision, in a microwave oven or on a hot plate. As you prepare the recipe, have children notice the colors and designs on the packaging for the Mexican food. How do the colors and designs compare with those found in the book?

**Meatless Tacos**

2 cans of refried beans

12 taco shells

lettuce, shredded

tomatoes, chopped

black olives, sliced (optional)

cheddar cheese

salsa (taco sauce)

Heat refried beans in a pot on the hot plate (stirring frequently), or for two minutes on "high" in the microwave. Spoon refried beans into the bottom of each taco shell. Warm in microwave for one minute on "high." (This is not a necessary step, but if a microwave is available, the taco shells do taste better warmed.) Into filled shells, place lettuce, tomatoes and olives. Spoon on salsa and grate cheese over the top. (Makes approximately 12 tacos.)

## Retell the Story with Puppets

Read aloud the book summary for *Borreguita and the Coyote* found on the book's dust cover flap. Have the children note that the author is *retelling* the story which means that she did not make the story up, but rather she heard the story from someone or somewhere else, and is now rewriting the story in her own words. Offer the children the opportunity to retell the story in their own words. Provide the children with copies of the puppet patterns found on page 67. Before cutting the patterns out, have children glue the entire page to construction paper. Decorate the lamb with glued-on cotton balls and the coyote with glued-on strands of grey yarn. Markers and glued-on felt scraps may be used to add more details to the puppets. Let puppets dry, then cut out. You or another adult can then use sharp scissors to cut finger holes in each puppet. Encourage children to refer to illustrations in the book in order to use puppets to retell the story of *Borreguita and the Coyote* in their own style.

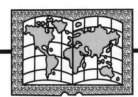

# Borreguita and the Coyote

lamb

cut out   cut out

coyote

cut out   cut out

# The Silver Whistle

by Ann Tompert
(Macmillan, 1988. 32 pp.)

*Miguel, a boy from Oaxaca, Mexico, is traveling to town with his family for the annual Christmas festival. Miguel hopes to buy a silver whistle to present to the Infant Jesus at the culminating Procession of Gifts. But, when Miguel's heart is tempted to help someone in need, he sabotages his own plans, and learns a great lesson about what gift-giving really means.*

## Before Reading *The Silver Whistle*

❍ Show students the book's illustrations—especially the series of illustrations depicting the festival. Help children to understand that a festival is a celebration with demonstrations (shows), foods for feasting and crafts for display and sale. Have the children describe exactly what they see in the very busy pictures. Ask if anyone in the class has ever been to a fair or festival. How did it compare to the festival pictured in the book?

## After Reading *The Silver Whistle*

❍ After listening to the story, ask the children to tell again what is similar to and what is different from the festivals the students have experienced. Help children understand that the festival in *The Silver Whistle* is a *religious* festival. Have any of the children in class attended religious festivals? Encourage discussion and sharing of experiences they may have had there.

FOLLOW-UP ACTIVITIES

## Used Toy Drive

Miguel is a boy who acts unselfishly toward others. Have the children recount all of the unselfish acts Miguel performs in the course of the story—especially for those less fortunate than he. Then, suggest that the class hold a "Used Toy Drive" to benefit children at a local hospital or day care center. Send a note home asking that children be allowed to select one of their own toys or books in good, clean condition to offer to the cause. If possible, arrange with the receiving facility to have the children deliver the toys in person to the recipients. Talk with the children about how difficult it was to give away a belonging, and how they felt once the donation was made.

## Clay Treasures

At the conclusion of *The Silver Whistle*, Miguel's modest clay bird (a gift he fashioned on his own) was the gift that most pleased The Holy One. In the art center, offer the children clay which is easy to mold and is able to air-dry. Also, provide the children with tools (e.g., rolling pins, cookie cutters, plastic knives, forks, clay hammers, etc.) for manipulating the clay. Tell children that they are free to use their clay to make a small statue as Miguel did, or to make a clay "cookie" which can be used to make a pendant. (Before drying clay pendants, remind children to use a small implement to pierce a hole to allow a ribbon "necklace" to be threaded through the top when dry.) Have children paint their clay creations. When dry, wrap each in a small piece of colorful tissue and have children present to someone they love.

## Special Gifts for Special People

In *The Silver Whistle,* Miguel's plans to present the Infant Jesus with a beautiful-looking gift are waylaid by his generosity to the people he meets on his way to the gift-giving ceremony. The storyline emphasizes that the best gifts are not necessarily those that are materially beautiful, but those that represent a generosity of heart and spirit. To help children better understand this concept, offer each child a copy of activity page 70. In the left-hand column, have students list the names (or draw the faces) of special people in their lives. Then, in the right-hand column, have students jot down meaningful, non-material gifts they would give to each person. Stress that the gifts should be personal in nature (i.e., suited to each recipient) and should represent a caring gift of self (e.g., a gift of time, a thoughtful deed done, a day-brightener, a promise made and kept, etc.). If desired, clip the "gifts" apart, glue to rectangular oaktag "mats" cut with pinking shears, decorate with markers and ribbon (see diagram below) and present as book marks to the special people for whom they were intended.

# The Silver Whistle

## Special People

## Special Gifts

# Ibrahim

by Francesc Sales
(J.B. Lippincott, 1989. 32 pp.)

*Ibrahim is looking forward to working at his father's stall in the marketplace of Marrakesh until Ibrahim's friend, Hassan, tells of his plan to leave the marketplace and live as a nomad in the desert. At once, life in the marketplace seems restrictive and dull. Life as a nomad seems exciting and free. How Ibrahim learns to satisfy both his longing to be free and his need to belong makes for a delightful tale.*

## Before Reading *Ibrahim*

○ Tell students that the main character in this book, Ibrahim, is faced with a dilemma. Ask them to listen carefully while you read the book to see if they can discover and understand Ibrahim's problem.

## After Reading *Ibrahim*

○ Ask for volunteers to summarize Ibrahim's problem in their own words. Have the students discuss whether or not Ibrahim solved his problem, and if so, then how did he do it? Ask: What did Ibrahim's father want him to do with his life? Do students believe that wanting children to stay close and follow in their parents' footsteps is only a Moroccan custom, or do other parents feel this way? Encourage support for reasoning. Can the children cite other examples (from real life or from literature) of instances when parents want their children to live a certain way?

> ## FOLLOW-UP ACTIVITIES

## Speculate on Linguistics

Locate Morocco on the map and notice its proximity to Spain. Inform the class that *Ibrahim* had to be translated from a language known as Catalan, a language spoken in Catalonia, a region located in the northeast of Spain. Ask students to make a list speculating why a story set in Morocco would be written in a language originating in Spain. (To assist students in their hypothesizing, share with them the "Translator's Notes" which appear on the book's end papers after the story text.) Inform students that people who study how language develops, spreads and changes are called *linguists*.

## Create a Marrakesh Marketplace

Students may be surprised to learn that in markets like the one in the book, prices are not fixed, but may be reduced by bargaining. For dramatic play, help students set up a marketplace in the classroom. You may want to hold a class flea market to raise funds for charity or school supplies once students get the feel of their "mock Marrakesh market." Study the illustrations in the book to see how an outdoor marketplace is both different from and similar to a supermarket or shopping mall. Stock your marketplace with baskets, dried or artificial flowers, bowls, and fruits and vegetables. Have children make simple craft projects that can be "sold" back to the creators in the market. (e.g., Decorate small clay pots using permanent markers or use strips of construction paper to weave paper placemats.) Provide scarves for the girls to wear and caps for the boys to wear. Have the children sew reusable shopping bags from felt or fabric scraps, or provide children with small paper bags with handles. You also might want to plan a special treat for the children to "buy" at the marketplace and eat during snacktime.

## Sequence Story Segments

The story *Ibrahim* contains many twists and turns in its story line making it easy for young readers to become confused by the turn of events. Offer students copies of the activity sheet on page 73 which recounts the events in the book and also has two blank spaces for students to recount other events of their own choosing. Have students cut apart story segments and place in sequential order as they occurred in the story. Then, have students use a pencil to number the events in the spaces provided. Students should refer to the book to check their work. Provide students with a supply of $8\frac{1}{2}'' \times 11''$ paper that has been cut in half horizontally. Instruct students to glue one story segment on each paper and illustrate, if desired. Staple booklets to bind.

# Ibrahim

Ibrahim becomes a storyteller in the marketplace.

Ibrahim has a dream that nomad riders on camels come to take him to the desert—which turns out to be more beautiful than he imagined.

Hassan tells Ibrahim that he hates the marketplace and plans to travel through the mountains to the desert.

Ibrahim begins working with his father in the Marrakesh marketplace.

Ibrahim talks with his father about leaving the marketplace to live in the desert.

The genie of the well appears to Ibrahim and tells him how to be happy.

Hassan leaves with his uncle.

# Tonight Is Carnaval

by Arthur Dorros
(Dutton Children's Books, 1991. 24 pp.)

*This upbeat book, about a Peruvian child anxiously awaiting Carnaval, is warmly illustrated with a series of folk-art quilts known as* arpilleras. *The story line introduces young readers to a slice of life in the Andes Mountains. An overview of a typically difficult work day is softened by the optimism of the colorful arpilleras—and by the promise of the Carnaval celebration to come!*

## Before Reading *Tonight Is Carnaval*

O Locate Peru on a topographical map. Help the children notice that much of Peru is located in the Andes Mountains. Use an encyclopedia to share pictures of Peru and the Andes with the class. Tell the class that they are going to hear a story that tells of a typical day for the Peruvians who live in the mountains-and of a special celebration that the people are looking forward to.

## After Reading *Tonight Is Carnaval*

O Ask the children to describe, in their own words, what life in the Andes must be like. Explain that Carnaval is one of the few celebrations that these hard-working people take part in. Ask the children if any of them would trade their lives for the way of life described in the story. Do the students believe that the people of Peru would want to change places with them? Why or why not? (Remind students that, despite the amount of work he is expected to do, the young narrator of the book does not sound unhappy about his life.)

FOLLOW-UP ACTIVITIES

## Appreciate Arpilleras

The quilts known as *arpilleras*, which are used to illustrate *Carnaval*, help readers understand the Peruvian way of life by offering a look at a popular regional folk-art form. Have children look at the photographs of the arpillera-makers quilting the wall-hangings together. Have them notice the modest workroom where the quilters are working, as well as the photograph of the woman working with her baby slung on her back. Read the photo captions to the class. Then, take a second look at each of the arpilleras used to illustrate the book. List all of the elements in each of the illustrations that tell us a bit about life in Peru (e.g., type of animals, work, instruments, terrain, vehicles, plants, etc.). Remind the children that any art form draws from the experience of the artists. Since arpilleras are popular decorating items, it may be possible to locate a real arpillera to share with the class. (Try borrowing one from a parent, a colleague or a local shop).

## Explore Folk Instruments

The narrator of the book looks forward to playing his *quena* (a reed flute) in the Carnaval band. Call attention to the glossary (located in the back of the book). Have a music teacher or musician bring in and demonstrate similar instruments to those pictured (making certain to include a reed instrument, a wind instrument and a percussion instrument). Why do the children believe the folk instruments of Peru are made of different materials than the instruments we are most familiar with? Your local record store may be able to help you select recordings of traditional Peruvian music you can bring in and play for the class.

## Sew an Arpillera

Use the patterns on page 76 to help the children make their own versions of an arpillera. For each arpillera you will need a piece of light blue felt (9″ × 12″), enough felt or fabric scraps to cut out the patterns pictured, needles, embroidery floss, yarn, cotton batting or polyester fiberfill and scissors. Pin the patterns to the fabrics and cut out. Then, pin the fabric shapes (backed by a bit of batting or fiberfill) to the felt background (as indicated in the illustration below). Show children how to use an overcast stitch or a running stitch to sew the pieces to the felt. For each piece of fruit, cut fabric circles from the pattern provided. Sew a running stitch around the circumference of each circle. Place a small ball of fiberfill in the center of each circular piece of fabric, and pull the thread tight to form a little fabric ball. Tack or glue the fruit ball to a leaf shape. Then, tack or glue the fruit and leaf to the tree. To finish the arpillera, use an overcast stitch or a running stitch to bind the edges of the felt.

Blanket stitch

Sew running stitch around edge of fruit circle pattern.

Stuff and pull tight to create fruit ball.

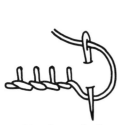

Leaf

flat circle fruit

**Hint:** fruit circles may be trimmed to create slightly smaller circles. These flat circles may then be tacked to leaves with or without stuffing.

Name _____

# Tonight Is Carnaval

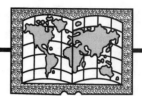

Arpillera Pattern Pieces

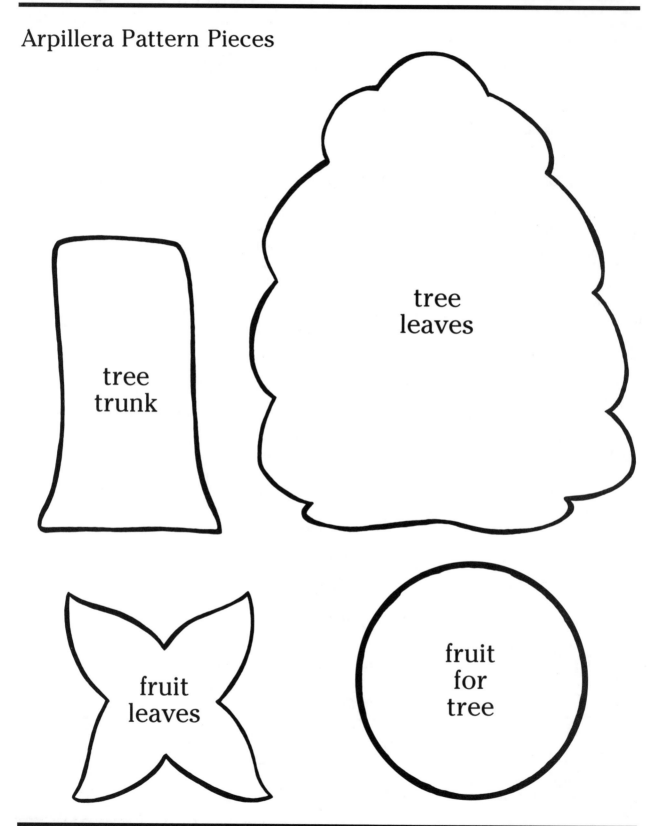

tree leaves

tree trunk

fruit leaves

fruit for tree

# Here Comes the Cat!

by Frank Asch and Vladimir Vagin
(Scholastic, 1989. 32 pp.)

*This story, about a big cat who comes to a community of mice, represents the first artistic and literary collaboration between an American and a Russian. Designed by popular American author/illustrator Frank Asch, and painted by Russian artist Vladimir Vagin,* Here Comes the Cat! *reinforces the old message that "all we have to fear is fear itself." The book, which is written in both English and Russian, helps to underscore how unfair and faulty negative prejudice can be.*

## Before Reading *Here Comes the Cat!*

❍ Have the children talk about times they may have worried about something that *might* happen. Is this any different from worrying about an occurrence that has already taken place or is definitely in the future? How?

## After Reading *Here Comes the Cat!*

❍ What were the mice worried about? Why were they so worried? Why was the story's ending a surprise?

| FOLLOW-UP ACTIVITIES |
| --- |

## Connecting Prejudice and Fear

Have the children explain how fear is spread in the story (e.g., by word of mouth). Introduce the word "prejudice" into the conversation. Help the children to understand that the word "prejudice" has to do with prejudging. Then, help students make the important connection between prejudice and fear by printing the following diagram on the blackboard or on a chart pad:

| Things some people don't like before they experience them. | What they're afraid of. |
| --- | --- |
| flying in an airplane | |
| snakes | |
| spinach | |
| broccoli | |

Have students tell what fear is associated with each item (e.g., students may fear tasting broccoli because it is a green vegetable or students may fear snakes because they think they are slimy). Ask how many of the items were actually experienced by the students, and how many were prejudged.

## Book Collaboratives

Explain to the class that the book's collaboration between a Russian and an American is an incredible achievement because for many years a "cold war" existed between the two powers, with each side regarding the other as an enemy. Help the class understand that a cold war is largely a war of words—with both sides fearing and mistrusting the other side. Invite students to create their own collaborative books based on the format of *Here Comes the Cat!* One or more students may write the text, while one or more other students may act as illustrators, interpreting the text with accompanying art work.

## Bilingual Dialogue Balloons

Provide students with copies of activity page 79 which features dialogue balloons and simple suggested messages to record in English and translate into other languages. In the space provided in each balloon, have students print the same message in a foreign language. In order to secure translations, students may ask for help from bilingual family members, or you may consider having foreign language teachers visit your class to assist with translations and pronunciations. You may also have children consult English/foreign language dictionaries. Staple completed dialogue balloons to a bulletin board covered with paper. Encourage the children to draw or paint characters near the balloons so that the characters appear to be speaking to each other.

# Here Comes the Cat

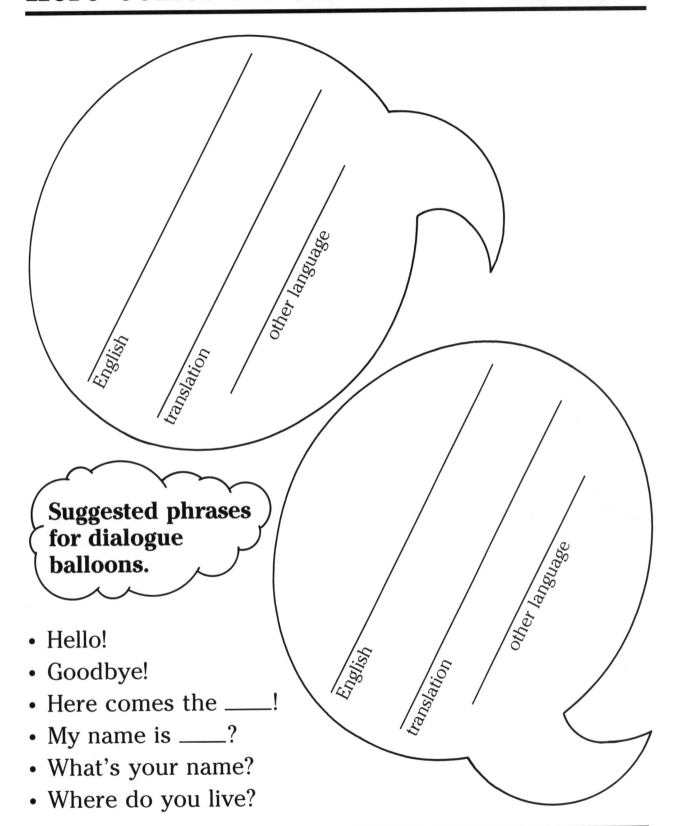

English

translation

other language

English

translation

other language

**Suggested phrases for dialogue balloons.**

- Hello!
- Goodbye!
- Here comes the ___!
- My name is ___?
- What's your name?
- Where do you live?

# Supergrandpa

by David Schwartz
(Lothrop, Lee and Shepard, 1991. 32 pp.)

*Gustav Hakansson was sixty years old when he decided to enter the* Sverige-Loppet, *the longest bicycle race in the history of Sweden. But the judges thought Hakansson too old to cycle the more than 1,000 mile course, so they barred him from entering the race. Defying the judges, Hakansson unofficially entered the race and went on to place first!*

## Before Reading *Supergrandpa*

❍ Help the class to understand that people in different cultures have different ideas about the role of older people. Some cultures venerate age, for example. In our own culture, not too long ago, grandparents (or older people) were often seen as too feeble to continue working or exercising—even if the older people wanted to continue working or exercising, they were forced to "take it easy" and/or retire. Today, older people are living longer, working longer and are encouraged to exercise and stay active as long as they can. Ask the children to tell of older people they know who are still working and exercising. (Because children's perceptions of what constitutes "old" may differ from an adult's, you may want to introduce the topic by first talking about the children's definition of "old.")

## After Reading *Supergrandpa*

❍ Have students tell why or why not the judges should have allowed Gustaf to enter the bicycle race (remembering that the judges could not have known how well Gustaf would perform). Even though Gustaf didn't *officially* win the race, he did come in first. Ask the children to explain how Gustaf's victory was a victory for older people everywhere.

## FOLLOW-UP ACTIVITIES

## Cycle across Sweden

Place a stationary exercise bicycle in the classroom. Post a large map of Sweden on the wall near the bicycle. Have children take turns logging miles on the bike in an attempt to cycle as far as Gustaf did (more than 1000 miles plus an extra 600 miles to represent the amount Gustaf cycled to arrive at the starting line at Haparanda). Have the group estimate how long it will take them to go the distance. Post a running total of miles logged by the class. Was 1,600 miles more or less than they imagined and predicted? Consider helping the class convert the mileage to metric kilometers (the method of measurement used in Sweden). After children are done cycling, offer them a snack of fruit soup and rye bread (recipe follows).

### Try Swedish Fruit Soup With Swedish Rye Bread
### Swedish Fruit Soup

One cup each of pear, peach, and plum juice (from canned fruit)
One cup each of orange and grapefruit **or** cranberry juice
    (prepared from concentrate or bottled)
$\frac{1}{4}$ teaspoon ground cinnamon
$\frac{1}{8}$ teaspoon ground cloves
6 canned plums
1 canned peach
1 canned pear
1 tablespoon cornstarch

Combine all the juices (except for $\frac{1}{4}$ cup of any juice) and spices
in a saucepan. Place over low heat, and simmer for one hour, stirring
occassionally. While the liquid mixture is cooking, coarsely chop the plums,
peach and pear. Add to the liquid mixture and bring to a boil. Combine
the cornstarch with the reserved $\frac{1}{4}$ cup of juice and stir to liquefy, then
add to the mixture to thicken. Stir to dissolve the cornstarch, and boil for
approximately ten minutes, being careful not to let the mixture burn. Yields
approximately 5 cups of soup. Serve hot or cold with a side dish of rye
bread and butter for a typical Swedish snack.

### Exercise Graph

Use the activity sheet on page 82 to help children discover favorite physical
activities of the older people in their lives. Along the bottom of the graph are
noted some common physical activities adults engage in. There is also room
for children to record (with words or small illustrations) additional physical
activities, sports, exercises, etc. that older people enjoy. Have children ask
adults they know to record their names above the activities in which they
participate. Adults may "vote" for more than one activity. Synthesize each
individual graph into one large graph by covering a bulletin board with craft
paper and drawing a grid directly on the paper. Ask if the children are
surprised to see how active the older people in their lives are.

### Elder/Younger Activities

Invite children to tell about activities they participate in with older friends
and relatives-such as playing catch, being pushed on a swing, digging in
sand or swimming at the beach. Have children draw pictures of themselves
and their older friends or relatives as they participate in these activities. If
you have the facilities near your school, you may want to have a "Super
Grandma/Grandpa Field Day." Have children create invitations to send to
their grandparents, asking them to come to school for a day of Grandparent-
Grandchild activities. You and the class can decide what these will be—egg-
and-spoon races, for example, or simple relay races, or other games of skill.
The children can make ribbons to be awarded for achievement in the
various activities.

# Supergrandpa

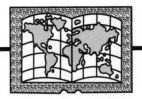

## Exercise Graph

Have your favorite adults vote for their favorite exercise by placing their names in the boxes above the exercise.

| Walking | Swimming | Dancing | Stretching | Bicycling | | |
|---------|----------|---------|------------|-----------|---|---|
| | | | | | | |
| | | | | | | |

# Rechenka's Eggs

by Patricia Polacco
(Philomel Books, 1988. 30 pp.)

*Babushka is known throughout all of Moskva for her beautifully painted eggs.
She also has an eye for the wonders of nature, so it is no surprise when she
befriends an injured goose she names Rechenka. But, when Rechenka turns
over a basket of Babushka's specially prepared eggs, the reader is surprised by
another wonder that saves the day!*

## Before Reading *Rechenka's Eggs*

❍ Ask the children if any of them have ever dyed or decorated eggs. Tell the
class that this story is about a woman who uses the Ukrainian art of egg
painting to prepare beautiful eggs for an Easter festival. Locate the Ukraine
on a map. If possible, show children a book which features the history and
photographs of this art form.

## After Reading *Rechenka's Eggs*

❍ Ask the children to describe what kind of person Babushka is. Use a
chart pad to record adjectives designed to paint a personality profile. Have
the children substantiate their opinions with passages from the text.

### FOLLOW-UP ACTIVITIES

## Observe "Onion Domes"

Have the children review the illustrations in the book to note the
architecture featured. Pay particular attention to the "onion domes" of
the large city buildings. Show children pictures of the Kremlin in Moscow,
and the White House in Washington, D.C.. How do the two structures
compare in appearance? Ask children if they think they can spot the
influence of such architecture in their own community. (Often, Russian
Orthodox churches will feature such influence.) Take a walk to notice what
other types of architecture are most prevalent in your community. If possible,
invite an architect or architectural student to accompany you, or take photos
of various buildings, and prepare a list of questions (regarding the features of
local architecture and the "onion domes" of Russia and the Ukraine) to
pose to your guest at a later date. Also, if your class has a "block corner,"
provide children with empty paper towel or empty tissue paper rolls and clay
and challenge them to incorporate "onion domes" into their block buildings.

## Egg-citing Decorations

Research to discover different ways to decorate egg shells. Visit a local craft
store and begin experimenting with various media and techniques (e.g.,
commercial egg-dying kits, paints, markers, decoupage, etc.). Students who
are used to decorating Easter eggs can help those who aren't. Allow each
child a chance to decorate a number of eggs. Create an "egg-tree" by having
them glue ribbons to the ends of the eggs and hanging their creations on

bare branches (available from craft stores, or gleaned from the ground in parks) which have been placed in soil or sand in flower pots. To complete egg trees, tie a ribbon on the end of each branch.

## Noting Nature's Wonders

In *Rechenka's Eggs*, part of the charm of main character, Babushka, is that she takes time to notice "miracles" or unexplainable events that someone else might easily take for granted, while part of the charm of the story line is that Babushka responds to all of these events—whether of fact or fantasy—with the same sense of wonderment. Provide each student with one copy of page 85. Then, have children reread the book in order to record each "miracle" Babushka notices (e.g., the caribou visit, Rechenka's eggs for the festival, caribou mothers and calves, Rechenka's gosling). Have children discuss whether they would classify these happenings as Babushka does, as "miracles". Have the children also discuss whether each natural occurrence would be likely to happen where they live. Then, have the children think of their own surroundings and jot in some natural "miracles" that occur in their own environment.

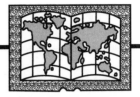

# Rechenka's Eggs

| Babushka's Miracles | True | Not True |
|---|---|---|
|  |  |  |
|  |  |  |
|  |  |  |
|  |  |  |

| Miracles That Happen Where _____ Lives |
| Student's Name |
|---|
|  |
|  |
|  |
|  |
|  |

# Tuan
by Eva Boholm-Olsson
(R&S Books, 1988. 24 pp.)

*Young readers will enjoy learning how Tuan, a Vietnamese boy, spends a typical day in his village. When Tuan is bitten by a rabid dog, readers can begin to appreciate the difficulties that such village life poses to the people who live there. And, when Tuan and his mother attend a children's festival, readers will easily identify with the universal laughter and fun such a celebration generates.*

## Before Reading *Tuan*

❍ Leaf through the book and show the illustrations to the class. Ask the children to tell what elements in the illustrations let the children know that *Tuan* is a story set in a foreign country. What is it about the illustrations that invites us to read the book?

## After Reading *Tuan*

❍ Ask the children to tell if they think life in Vietnam (as depicted in the book) describes a way of life that is more similar to or more different from their own. What would happen to them if they had been bitten by a dog? Would they have to worry about getting the proper medicine?

### FOLLOW-UP ACTIVITIES

## Learning More About Vietnam

Locate Vietnam on a map. From the illustrations and text, can the class determine the climate of Vietnam? Research the country in the encyclopedia to discover that the country is located in a very hot and humid zone, and that much of the country is covered in jungle. How does the class believe such terrain and climate affect the way people live, work and play?

## Places to Go, Things to Do

Have the children imagine that Tuan is coming to visit with them. Provide each child with a copy of the activity on page 87. In the space provided on the top half of the page, have each child make a list of places and experiences he or she would share with Tuan if he came to visit. Next to each item, have each child explain why he or she chose to include the item on his or her list. Have students repeat the exercise on the lower half of the page, this time having children note places and experiences he or she would like to share if visiting Tuan in Vietnam. Again, have each child explain why he or she chose the items on his or her list. Use the activity to help children understand that experiences which differ from the familiar are often the most enjoyable and educational.

Author Eva Boholm-Olsson lived in Vietnam and the characters in her book *Tuan* are based on people she met there. Illustrator Pham Van Don is a popular artist in Vietnam.

Name _____

# Tuan

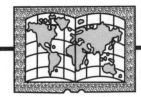

| Places and Experiences I would share with Tuan if he visited me: | Reasons Why . . . |
|---|---|
| | |
| | |
| | |
| | |
| | |
| Places and Experiences I would like to share if I visited Tuan in Vietnam | Reasons Why . . . |
| | |
| | |
| | |
| | |

## Ghanaian

# Amoko and Efua Bear

by Sonia Appiah
(Macmillan, 1988. 28 pp.)

*Amoko Efua Mould lives in Ghana, West Africa. Her middle name, Efua, means that she was born on a Friday. Amoko is sure that her favorite toy, a little stuffed bear, was born on a Friday, too, so she named her Efua Bear. Usually Efua Bear is first in Amoko's heart, but when Amoko receives a gift of a toy drum from her aunt she is so excited about the new toy that she accidently leaves her beloved bear in the yard overnight. The story allows young readers to feel close to Amoko and her predicament, even though she lives in far-away Ghana.*

## Before Reading *Amoko and Efua Bear*

❍ Ask the class to tell if any of them have favorite dolls, puppets or stuffed animals that are special to them. (Older children who may not still feel an attachment to such a toy [or who might be reluctant to admit such an attachment in class] can tell about toys they used to care about when they were little.) Locate Ghana on a map or globe. Tell the class that this is a story about a girl from Ghana and the little stuffed animal that she cared about—even though the girl did forget about her stuffed bear for one whole night.

## After Reading *Amoko and Efua Bear*

❍ Ask the children to tell about times they may have forgotten a favorite toy. Ask them how they felt, and then have them look at the picture of Amoko that shows how she felt when she discovered Efua was missing. Have them describe what she might be feeling. Ask the children to explain how their feelings could be so similar to those of a child who lives so far away.

---

### FOLLOW-UP ACTIVITIES

---

## Same/Different Card Game

To help children understand how much they have in common with Amoko and her life in Ghana, use a pack of index cards to create a set of same/different game cards. For each set of cards, make a copy of the statements on page 90. (The statements presented are based on the book's illustrations.) Cut the statements apart and glue each on a separate index card. Have children take turns sorting the cards into two piles representing ways they are the *same* as Amoko and ways they are *different* from Amoko. After all the children have had a chance to sort and count their two piles of cards, have them discuss whether they were surprised to discover they have a lot in common with a girl from such a faraway place.

## Toys to School

Invite the children to bring to school their favorite stuffed animal or doll to share with the class. To promote some creative communication, assemble the children in a circle and direct interview questions at the toys. Find out the toys' names and how they came to live with their people. Remind toys of how Amoko includes Efua Bear in all of her play, and ask them to tell of any games they play(ed) with their children. Ask them what they like to eat and to describe where they live. After each toy has had a chance to respond, try grouping the toys according to various criteria (e.g., color, size, type, etc.). Consider graphing your information on a floor graph (made with markers on craft paper or with chalk on a concrete or blacktop surface outdoors). Have children place toys directly on the graph as suggested in the illustration below.

## Write "Otherwise" Books

Remind children what happened when Amoko forgot her responsibility for Efua Bear. Then, have students brainstorm a list of responsibilities they have at home and a second list of responsibilities they have at school. Record these on a chart pad. Then, have children create a corresponding "otherwise" list of consequences for not fulfilling these responsibilities. (For example, we hang up our coats in the closet, otherwise, the coats fall on the floor and become tangled and dirty.) Have children refer to the list to create their own "otherwise" books. Provide paper for the children to record and illustrate their ideas as illustrated below. Staple completed pages between sheets of construction paper and share finished books with the group.

# Amoko and Efua Bear

| | |
|---|---|
| Amoko takes a bath outside using buckets of water. | Amoko carries her bear tied to her back. |
| Amoko sees a lizard sunning on a wall. | Amoko drinks milk from a coconut. |
| Amoko helps her parents make dinner. | Amoko likes to play hide-and-seek. |
| Amoko likes getting new toys. | Amoko feels sad when her bear is hurt. |

# Amazing Grace

by Mary Hoffman
(Dial Books for Young Readers, 1991. 25 pp.)

*Grace is a girl who loves to hear stories and then act out the most exciting parts. Grace learns that her class is about to stage the play* Peter Pan, *and she knows just which part she wants to play. But, when she raises her hand to try out for the part of Peter, Grace's classmates tell her she can't play the part because she's a girl and because she's black. With encouragement from those who love her most, Grace manages to land the part of Peter, and in doing so, proves that she is able to fly above limitations imposed by others.*

## Before Reading *Amazing Grace*

❍ Ask the children to talk about their favorite pretend games. Do they play different pretend games when they are together than when they are alone? Tell the class that this book is about a girl named Grace who loves to pretend that she is the characters she reads about in books.

## After Reading *Amazing Grace*

❍ Ask the class to tell what kind of girl they think Grace is. Is she the type of girl they'd like to know and play with? Why or why not? When Grace's classmates told her she could not play the part of Peter Pan because she was black and because she was a girl, Grace didn't seem bothered by their words and she still tried out for the part. But, once she was home, she told her family how upset she was. What does this tell us about the kind of girl Grace is?

## FOLLOW-UP ACTIVITIES

## Watch *Peter Pan*

Have the class view the video film of *Peter Pan* starring Mary Martin as Peter Pan. Point out to the class that the role of Peter Pan is being played by a woman. Point out also that the part of Tiger Lily is not being played by a Native American. Encourage children to discuss whether they think that these parts should always be be played by a boy and a Native American? Why or why not? (Students might be interested to learn that hundreds of years ago, all the roles in Shakespeare's plays, for example, were played by men—even the roles of women—because women weren't allowed to be actors.) Why does the class think that Grace wanted the role of Peter? Have the students imagine which parts they would each like to play and tell why.

## Create "Caring Manuals"

Have the students examine the illustrations involving Grace's family. From the faces on the characters of Ma and Nana, and from the way these two women are shown relating to Grace, (hugging her, holding her hand, playing with her), have the students imagine how Grace's family members feel about each other. Have the children take turns describing simple ways to show caring for friends and family. (Stress that showing we care needs not always involve traditional gift-giving.) Then, have each class member make a list (or a series of illustrations) depicting ways they show they care for others (i.e., family members or friends). Suggest that children use their lists and illustrations to create "Caring Manuals" containing ideas for showing that they care. Have children share their manuals with the group. How many separate ideas was the class able to generate? Consider recording these (as a constant reminder to care) on a display chart in the classroom.

## Pretend Props

Have the children search through the illustrations of Grace play-acting to discover the props and play costumes she used in each of her pretend games. List these on a large chart pad for the children to refer to (e.g., "Grace used scarves to look like Anancy the Spider."). Provide each of the children with a copy of activity page 93 which suggests roles they could play-act. Then, have the children search in the classroom or at home to find articles of clothing and other items they could use to create a pretend costume for the role they chose. Children should illustrate and label their ideas in the space provided. Consider setting time aside for children to dress in their original costume designs, and, if appropriate, dance or act out their characters. Take photos of the children in costume and post these on a bulletin board next to the children's illustrations. Allow time for children to explain how they created their costumes.

| Joan of Arc | belt, large shirt, sword, shield |
| Anancy the spider | hat, stockings, striped shirt |
| Peter Pan | tights, belt sword, hat |
| C...... | ...ess, ribbons heels |

Name _____

# Amazing Grace

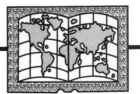

| Roles | Costumes and Props |
|---|---|
| Royalty<br><br>King, Queen,<br>Prince, or Princess | |
| Animal<br><br><br><br>_____<br>name specific type of animal | |
| T.V. or Movie<br>Character<br><br><br>_____<br>name of character | |
| Book Character<br><br><br><br>_____<br>name of character | |

# Ben's Trumpet

by Rachel Isadora
(Greenwillow Books, 1979. 32 pp.)

*With limited text and striking black and white art deco-inspired art, the author tells the story of a young boy in the 1920s who sits on his fire escape longing to play jazz music like he hears coming from the nearby "Zig Zag Jazz Club." Aside from introducing young readers to the instruments used to create jazz sounds, the book shows how one boy's artistic bent can feed a dream only another artist can truly understand.*

## Before Reading *Ben's Trumpet*

❍ Ask the children to talk about their favorite *types* of music. Invite children who understand about different types of music to share what they know with the group. Show the group the book, *Ben's Trumpet*. Ask the children to tell how the book looks different from other picture books they know (Possible responses: the pictures are in black and white, the illustrations are comprised of outlines, silhouettes and abstract designs).

## After Reading *Ben's Trumpet*

❍ Ask the children what problems Ben has in seeing his dream of playing jazz come true (e.g., He doesn't own an instrument; his friends make fun of him). Do they believe Ben will ever learn to play the trumpet? Why? Why doesn't Ben's family buy him a trumpet? (Remind children that in the 1920s many families didn't have much money to buy expensive things for their children.)

### FOLLOW-UP ACTIVITIES

## Jazz Intro

Help students to understand that, especially at the beginning of the jazz movement, most of the jazz musicians were African–American men. Tell the children that many of these musicians were not allowed to play in the musical clubs with white owners (or, even in those white-owned clubs where they were allowed, other black people were not allowed into the audience). So, they created their own jazz clubs, much like the "Zig Zag Jazz Club." If possible, invite a jazz musician (or music teacher) to visit your classroom to introduce the children to the instruments pictured in the book. Ask the musician to tell about the roots of jazz music, or share portions of the book *Jazz* by Langston Hughes (Franklin Watts, 1982). *Jazz* offers a brief history of jazz as well as mini-biographies of jazz greats. Also included is a glossary of jazz terms.

## Jazz-y Paintings

Point out to the children that the writer has chosen an art deco style of art (popular in the 1920s) to illustrate the book. Show the children art books featuring other examples of art deco works. Ask the children to describe how the artist used this style of art to make the book's illustrations "look like" the sounds of jazz music. Offer the children black tempera paint and white paper. Play selections of jazz music and have the children paint what they hear. Have children share their paintings and their reactions to the music. How does it differ from other music they know?

## Multicultural Music Festival

Use copies of the invitation on page 96 to invite students, teachers and parents to display their musical talents at a school-wide music festival. In addition to playing a selection of regional music, participating musicians should be prepared to explain the history, origin and mechanics of their instrument of choice to the students. Make every effort to include music representing various periods and styles as well as instruments emanating from a variety of cultures in your festival.

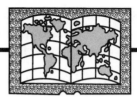

# Ben's Trumpet

## Students! Teachers! Parents! Please **Note** . . .

# Multicultural Music Festival
## Talent Search!

Here's your chance to display your musical talent at our school-wide Multicultural Music Festival to be held at _____ on
<small>place, time</small>

_____.
<small>date</small>

   If you're willing to donate your talents to sing or play a selection of regional music, please complete the following information and return to _____ by
<small>name</small>

_____.
<small>date</small>

- - - - - - - - - - - - - - - - - - - - - - - - - - - - - -

Yes, I would love to participate in the Multicultural Music Festival. For my performance, I plan to

_____. _____ / _____
                        **Name**        **Phone Number**

# Cornrows

by Camille Yarborough
(Coward, McCann & Geoghegan, Inc. 1979. 44 pp.)

*In a "story-within-a-story," this author tells of the significance that braiding hair into cornrows holds for African-Americans. The book underscores the power that symbolism holds for a culture, and offers a perfect starting point for exploring the symbolism present in other cultures.*

## Before Reading *Cornrows*

○ Show the class the illustrations and ask them what they notice. (The illustrations—soft, muted black and white sketches without edges—are meant to blend past and present into one dream, one reality for the people who share a heritage.) Point out how illustrations of the present overlap illustrations of ancient peoples and ask the children why the illustrator chose to present the artwork this way.

## After Reading *Cornrows*

○ Celebrate class unity by having the class make and eat Braided Bread, following the recipe below. You may want to start the yeast mixture and put the bread aside to rise before the class arrives, or have the children help you with it early in the day, as it needs 1½ to 2 hours to rise before it is ready to work. This is a wonderful group activity: children can help with measuring, mixing, kneading and shaping the loaves—and of course, all can share in the eating!

### Braided Bread

    3 packages active dry yeast
    1⅓ cups warm water (100° to 115°, approximately)
    1 tablespoon granulated sugar
    1 tablespoon coarse salt
    3 tablespoons softened butter
    3 eggs
    5 to 5½ cups all-purpose flour
    1 egg yolk mixed with one teaspoon cold water
    poppy seeds (optional)

Dissolve the yeast and sugar in ½ cup of the warm water in a large bowl. Stir well and set aside for a few minutes. The fermentation should become evident as the mixture swells and bubbles appear—if this does not happen, the yeast is not active: it must be discarded and the process begun again, with a new packet of yeast and the same quantities of water and sugar. If the yeast *is* active, add the salt, sugar, butter and eggs and the 5 cups of flour (one cup at a time). Beat thoroughly with a wooden spoon (children can help). The dough should be very stiff. Add up to ½ cup more flour, a little at a time, if it is not stiff enough. Turn the dough out onto a floured surface. Knead approximately 10 minutes. Children can take turns kneading (after they wash their hands) until the dough is smooth and elastic. Place the dough in a very large, well-oiled bowl, and turn it once to coat all the surfaces with oil. Cover and let rise 1½ to 2 hours in a warm, draft-free place until doubled in bulk. When doubled, punch down and divide into six equal parts. Roll each portion into a rope about 1 inch in diameter on a lightly floured surface. Braid 3 ropes together to make 2 loaves. Place about 6 inches apart on a well-oiled baking sheet. Cover and let rise again until almost doubled in bulk. Then brush the tops of the loaves with the egg yolk and water mixture and sprinkle with poppy seeds if desired. Bake in a preheated oven at 400° for 35 to 45 minutes. Cool completely before sharing with the class.

## FOLLOW-UP ACTIVITIES

### Cornrow Demonstration

Look on a map to find the places Mama mentions where people wore cornrows (i.e., Egypt, Swaziland, Senegal and Somali). Invite someone to your class to demonstrate how hair is braided into cornrows. Have children braid lengths of yarn together into bracelets to present to each other as a similar symbol of tightly woven friendships.

### Learning About VIP's

In the book, Mama lists people for whom the cornrows may be named (e.g., Robeson, Malcolm, Dr. King, DuBois, etc). Have students research these names to discover why they are significant to the African and African-American culture. Students may then report to the class on why these would be good people to honor with the symbolic hairstyle.

### Symbols and Traditions

Reread the page in the book that tells how it was possible to tell which clan or class people belonged to by the way their hair was braided. Ask the children to bring in examples of similar "wearable" symbols they're familiar with (e.g., sports' paraphernalia, scouting uniforms, school uniforms, buttons, native costumes, logo-laden tee shirts, caps, etc.). Use the form on page 99 to list such symbols and their significance. Ask: Why are such symbols important? (Possible answers: They unite people in a visible way; they make people feel as though they belong together, etc.)

Name _____

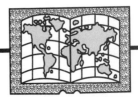

# Cornrows

| Symbols of Unity | Significance of Symbols |
|---|---|
|  |  |
|  |  |
|  |  |
|  |  |
|  |  |

# Everett Anderson's Goodbye

by Lucille Clifton
(Holt, Rinehart and Winston,
1983. 21 pp.)

*In simple, but elegant rhyme, the author shows a small boy's pain as he progresses through five predictable stages of grief in an effort to cope with his father's death. The story line is complemented by rich and tender black and white pencil sketches of Everett Anderson as he experiences emotions ranging from denial to acceptance. Together, the storyline and illustrations effectively evoke some of the feelings we all experience when we grieve.*

## Before Reading *Everett Anderson's Goodbye*

○ Show the class the illustrations in the book. Ask: What do you think the book is about? How do you think we will feel after reading the book?

## After Reading *Everett Anderson's Goodbye*

○ Ask the children for their reactions to the book. Ask the children to explain in their own words what Everett must be feeling inside. Even though the book doesn't tell us how Everett's mom is feeling, have the children speculate about her feelings. Have children volunteer to tell about times they've felt the same as Everett Anderson. Ask the children if they think it's ever wrong to feel sad or to cry as he did.

## FOLLOW-UP ACTIVITIES

## Exploring Ethnicity and Feelings

Use a chart pad or chalkboard to list the five stages of grief (located in the front of the book). Then, reread the book to discover how Everett behaves during each stage. (The stages are numbered in the text.) Ask the children if they think the story would be different if the character looked different from Everett (e.g., if the character was a girl or was not black). Help the children to notice that the setting isn't specified. Have the children speculate as to why the author and illustrator created a book that could take place almost anywhere. They may conclude that the main character's feelings are universal, too. Help the children to understand that doctors who study the science of how people think and feel (psychology) have learned that nearly everyone who is saddened by a death goes through the same five stages: They are universal, too.

## Collaborative Big Book

Reread the book (paying special attention to the illustrations) to discover what Everett's mother does to help him feel better. Ask each child to think of one way they help others when they are feeling sad. (Help children understand that it is not always necessary to "cheer up" a sad friend in an effort to help him or her. While sad feelings are uncomfortable, they sometimes help us accept things we cannot change and they are an inevitable, transitory part of life, not something wrong or bad.) List these helpful ideas on a chart pad, beginning each contribution with the sentence starter, "One good way to help someone who is feeling sad is. . ." Help children transfer each contribution to a large piece of construction paper or oaktag. Have children illustrate their own contributions. Bind pages together into a collaborative "Big Book of Helpful Hints for Helping Someone Who Feels Sad."

## Feelings in Common

To help children understand that, despite our differences, we all share feelings in common, provide each student with a copy of the activity on page 102. Review the emotions represented by the faces at the top of the page. Make certain that the children understand each emotion featured by having the class supply concrete examples of each from their own experiences (e.g., "I felt shy when. . ."). On the top half of the page, have the children read each of the situations and then check off the faces that tell how the situations would make them feel. Tell children that for each situation they may choose to check off more than one face (indicating that more than one feeling can be present at the same time). On the bottom half of the page, have students record an experience that makes them feel each of the the emotions indicated. Share the results of the activity. Did any of the children share feelings in common?

# Everett Anderson's Goodbye

## How do you feel When . . .

| | happy | sad | angry | embarrassed | worried | frightened | shy | surprised |
|---|---|---|---|---|---|---|---|---|
| 1. a classmate gives you a hug? | | | | | | | | |
| 2. it's the last day of school? | | | | | | | | |
| 3. you have to do a lot of homework? | | | | | | | | |
| 4. an adult says you're "so cute." | | | | | | | | |
| 5. someone else gets blamed for something you did. | | | | | | | | |

1. 😊 shy _____
2. 😠 angry _____
3. 😟 worried _____
4. 🙂 happy _____
5. 😳 embarrassed _____

# Flossie and the Fox

by Patricia C. McKissack
(Dial Books For Young Readers, 1986. 32 pp.)

*When Big Mama sends little Flossie Finley on an errand, Big Mama includes a warning to watch out for a sly, egg-poaching fox on the loose. But, Flossie doesn't know what a fox looks like, so when she runs into one on her way through the woods, she challenges him to prove he's for real! This folktale will delight readers who will fall in love with clever Flossie's indomitable spirit.*

## Before Reading *Flossie and the Fox*

○ Remind students that animals in literature are usually thought to have certain "stereotypic" qualities (e.g., pigs are sloppy and lazy, lions are courageous, mice are timid, lambs are gentle, rats are not to be trusted, etc.). Get children on the right train of thought by asking if they know what it means to be "chicken" or a "pig." Ask if any of the children have ever heard the expression, "sly as a fox." (If necessary, help children look up the exact meaning of the word "sly" in the dictionary.) Tell the children that this story is about a little girl who meets just such a sly fox on her way to a neighbor's house.

## After Reading *Flossie and the Fox*

○ Ask the children to describe what kind of a girl Flossie is. Have them cite examples from the book to support their reasonings By the end of the book, Flossie says she believes the fox is telling the truth. Ask students to explain when they believe Flossie first knew that the fox really *was* a fox.

### FOLLOW-UP ACTIVITIES

## Learning from Illustrations

Help the class define what is meant by a story's *setting* and *time*. Tell children that illustrations can sometimes help them understand where and when a story takes place. Have students look through the book's illustrations to locate clues that tell about where *Flossie and the Fox* takes place (a warm, rural, woodsy setting). Then, have them look for clues (e.g., clothing, toys) that help tell when (in time) the story takes place.

## Smart Decision-Making

When she meets up with the dangerous fox, Flossie relies on some quick thinking to keep herself safe. Provide each student with a copy of the activity on page 104. After reading each scenario, have the children imagine how they would react and what they would do if faced with the same or similar situation. Have them record their ideas in the space provided. Allow children time to share their problem solutions. (Children prone to "tunnel vision" will benefit from exposure to a variety of possible actions and reactions to the same situation.) For a twist on this activity, have children guess how classmates will respond before revealing answers. Also, imagine how Flossie would handle each situation.

# Flossie and the Fox

A strange dog runs up to you on the playground.

A stranger offers you candy.

Your friends want you to play at a construction site.

Your friends dare you to climb up to the top of the playground jungle gym and hang upside down by your knees.

You're home alone and a stranger knocks on the door.

# Follow the Drinking Gourd

by Jeanette Winter
(Alfred A. Knopf,
1988. 42 pp.)

*The complex system that led runaway African slaves to freedom is exquisitely portrayed in this easy-to-understand text about the Underground Railroad. Readers can't help but stand in awe of what slaves were forced to endure when in bondage—and what they were willing to risk to be free.*

## Before Reading *Follow the Drinking Gourd*

❍ Ask students to explain in their own words how much they know about slavery in our history. Use the opportunity to correct any misconceptions about slavery. Use a globe to show the class how slavers sailed from American shores to Africa and back, in order to capture Africans and force them to work on the southern plantations in the States. If possible, show the children a copy of *Roots* by Alex Haley (G.K. Hall & Co. 1976). Reading excerpts from the book will graphically illustrate to the students how slaves traveled on slave ships, and provide accurate historical information on the issue of slavery in America.

## After Reading *Follow the Drinking Gourd*

❍ Have students study the faces of the runaway slaves as illustrated in the book. Ask students to list all of the feelings they see on the characters' faces. Can the students imagine how they would have felt and what they would have done if they had been enslaved?

## FOLLOW-UP ACTIVITIES

## Musical Mapping

Help the class learn the "Follow The Drinking Gourd Song" as written in the back of the book. (If necessary, engage a music teacher's assistance in order to accurately decipher the musical score.) After the class has learned the song, reread the text, pausing to have the class sing the song segments. If desired, you may bridge the spoken and sung segments by providing light musical accompaniment (e.g., guitar chords, etc.) throughout the entire shared reading. With some practice, you may want to present a reading of the book, complete with song and instrumental accompaniment, to other classes.

Have the students skim the book to note all of the dangers the runaway slaves encountered on their way to freedom. Make a separate list of all of the hardships they endured while trying to escape. Then, have the children list what choices (besides running away) the slaves had if they wanted to live a free and happy life with their families. (The exercise should help the children realize that the slaves had no options but to stay and be treated cruelly or try to run away.) Help the children understand that the slaves' dark skin color was a hindrance to their escape because anywhere they went they could easily be identified and captured again. Encourage the children to discuss whether they think a person's skin color can make a difference in his or her life today.

## Map Out the Underground Railroad

Provide each of the students with a copy of the map on page 107. Refer to the page in the book entitled, "A Note About the Story." After reading the information to the class, use a chalkboard or chart pad to list the stops on Peg Leg Joe's legendary Undergound Railroad route. Have the children use an atlas of the United States to locate the places mentioned. Using the map shape on page 107 as a pattern, use an overhead projector to project and trace the shape onto a bulletin board covered with craft paper. As a group, have the class record the sites and the route of the Underground Railroad on the blank wall map. Have children draw or paint runaway slaves and Peg Leg Joe along the route. Have students then transfer this information to their individual maps, adding pictorial detail as desired. These maps may be used as covers for a collection of student book reports on *Follow the Drinking Gourd* and other African-American books.

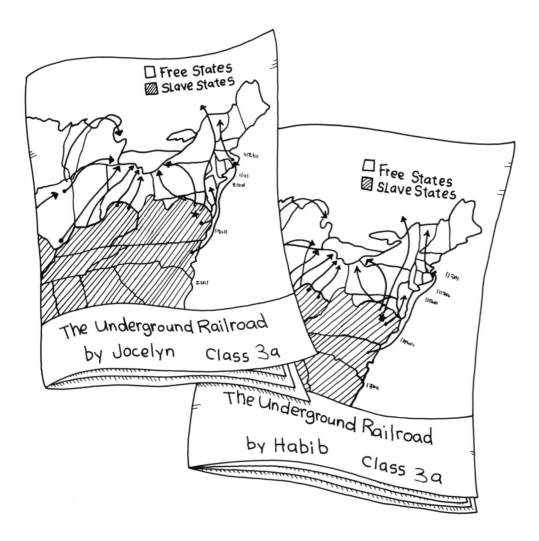

Name _____

# Follow the Drinking Gourd

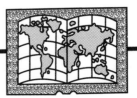

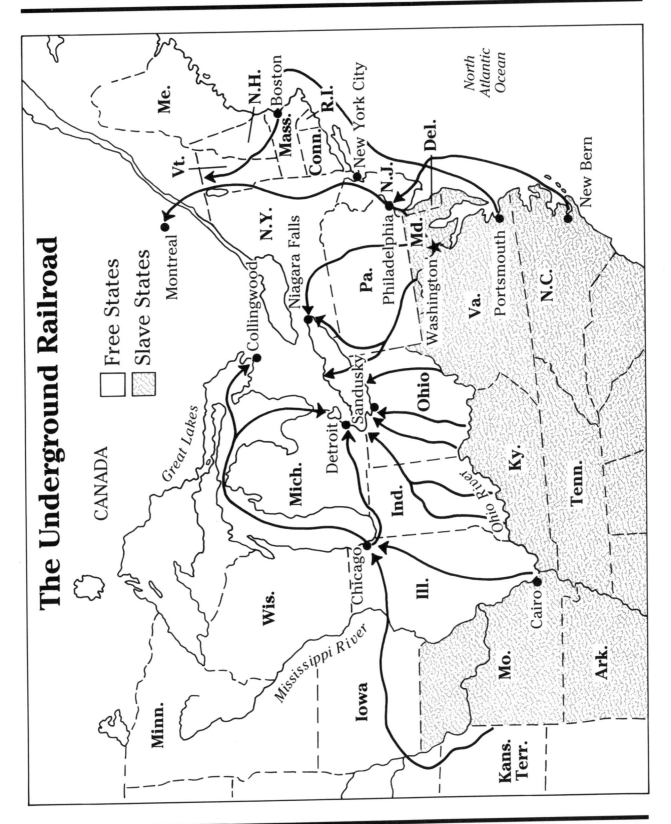

## The Underground Railroad

CANADA

☐ Free States
▨ Slave States

Great Lakes

Montreal

Collingwood

Detroit

Chicago

Sandusky

Niagara Falls

New York City

Boston

Philadelphia

Washington

Portsmouth

New Bern

North Atlantic Ocean

Mississippi River

Ohio River

Minn.

Wis.

Iowa

Ill.

Ind.

Mich.

Ohio

Pa.

N.Y.

Vt.

N.H.

Me.

Mass.

Conn.

R.I.

N.J.

Del.

Md.

Va.

N.C.

Ky.

Tenn.

Mo.

Ark.

Kans. Terr.

Cairo

# Me and Neesie

by Eloise Greenfield
(Thomas Y. Crowell Co. 1975. 33 pp.)

*Before Neesie came along, Janell was a lonely little girl who had no one to play with her. Neesie likes all of the same things as Janell. Of course, grown-ups can't see Neesie, but she behaves just like Janell, even getting into the same trouble as Janell. But, when it's time for Neesie to go to school, Janell doesn't want to come along... and young readers will probably understand why.*

## Before Reading *Me and Neesie*

❍ Tell the class that, in the book they are about to read, the main character named Janell has a make-believe friend named Neesie. Ask the children if any of them have ever had an imaginary or make-believe friend. Talk about the pros and cons of such a friendship. As they listen to the story, ask the children to be aware of the problems Neesie causes for Janell.

## After Reading *Me and Neesie*

❍ Ask the children to offer possible explanations for why Mama asks Janell not to tell Aunt Bea about Neesie. After getting to know Aunt Bea, do the children believe she would have been upset if she knew about Neesie? Why do the children believe Neesie didn't *want* to go to school?

## FOLLOW-UP ACTIVITIES

## Real Research on Imaginary Friends

Ask the class to hypothesize about imaginary friends—do they believe that children all over the world create imaginary playmates? Have the children discuss their reasoning. After taking a poll in your class regarding who believes that having imaginary friends is a universal phenomenon, post a simple sign-in chart as pictured below. Have any classroom visitors, with first-hand knowledge of whether or not imaginary friends exist in their culture or ethnic group, record their information on the chart.

## Friendly Comparisons

Remind children that Neesie and Janell looked and behaved almost identically. Help the class understand that we all enjoy being around friends with whom we have a lot in common—but that sometimes we have to get to know people to see how much alike we really are. Offer each student a copy of page 110 which will help them think about how they are alike and how they are different from their classmates. Begin by placing each of the students' names on a scrap of paper. To pair students randomly, divide the class in half and allow one half of the children to draw a classmate's name from a hat. Children should then record their names and the name of the classmate on the activity page. Review the criteria with the class, and instruct the children to fill in information about themselves accordingly.

Then, have them guess at how their classmate would respond to the same criteria. Have the children compare results to see how well they know each other, and how much alike they are. Repeat the pairing and comparing process as often as you like. Then, use the information recorded on the activity sheet to group children with common likes and dislikes. ("Everyone who likes pizza as their favorite food, stand here.") If desired, create individual graphs for each of your results.

Author Eloise Greenfield was born in Parmele, NC and grew up in Washington, DC, where she now lives. She has headed both the Adult Fiction and Children's Literature Divisions of the D.C. Black Writer's Workshop.

| Criteria | Carla Name | John Paul Classmate's Name |
|---|---|---|
| Favorite Food | Fried Chicken | Pizza |
| Favorite Color | Red | Green |
| Favorite Game | Tag | Monopoly |
| Favorite School activity or subject | Math | English |
| Favorite pet animal | Goldfish | Puppy |
| Favorite Music | Rock | Rap |
| Favorite Book | Sara, Plain & Tall | Me and Neesie |

# Me and Nessie

| Criteria | Name | Classmate's Name |
|---|---|---|
| Favorite food | | |
| Favorite color | | |
| Favorite game | | |
| Favorite school activity or subject | | |
| Favorite pet animal | | |
| Favorite music | | |
| Favorite book | | |

# Peter's Chair

by Ezra Jack Keats
(Harper & Row, 1967. 32 pp.)

*Peter's new baby sister, Suzie, seems to be taking over the whole house. Peter's mother tells him to play quietly because Suzie is napping. Father is painting Peter's old crib and highchair pink because they belong to Suzie now. When Peter spots his old chair, he decides to take the chair and run away so they won't give that to the baby, too! How Peter finally comes to volunteer to paint the little chair pink himself makes for a delightfully universal story about growing up.*

## Before Reading *Peter's Chair*

○ Find out how many of the children have younger brothers or sisters at home. Do they remember when their younger siblings were babies? Have the children take turns describing in as much detail as possible what it feels like to be jealous of the baby. What did they do when they felt jealous? Tell the group that they are going to learn a story about a boy who is jealous of his little sister.

## After Reading *Peter's Chair*

○ Have the children imagine all the reasons why Peter was jealous of Suzie (e.g., she got to use his crib and high chair, Mother and Father were paying lots of attention to Suzie, etc.). What made Peter change his mind about giving his chair to Suzie?

## FOLLOW-UP ACTIVITIES

## Bring 'n Brag Baby Pictures

When Peter leaves home, he takes his baby picture with him. Have the children examine Peter's baby picture and the illustration of Peter as he appears now. How are the two the same? How are they different? Provide each student with an envelope (discarded "junk mail" envelopes will do), and have the children use the envelopes to transport their own baby pictures, plus a recent snapshot, to school. Use a paper border or yarn to divide a bulletin board in half vertically. Post the baby pictures in a vertical line on one side of a bulletin board. Then, post the children's recent photos on the other side of the board. Have children take turns trying to use lengths of yarn to match the babies with the older children. As long as they guess correctly, allow each child to continue to try making matches. When a student guesses incorrectly, allow another student to have a turn. When all photo pairs have been correctly identified (and joined by lengths of yarn tacked to the board), ask children to notice physical features that are the same (e.g., hair color, skin color, etc.) and features that have changed (e.g., height, weight, etc.). What features do all the baby pictures and all the older children's pictures have in common, despite ethnicity? Can the children predict how they will appear in the future?

## Collage a Room Design

The author-illustrator uses collage materials to create the illustrations for *Peter's Chair*. Have the class examine the book page by page to see if they can identify the common materials Keats incorporated into the illustrations (e.g., wallpapers, lace doilies and newspaper). Provide the children with similar materials along with catalogs featuring housewares and furniture. Also, provide each student with a piece of lightweight cardboard or oaktag (approx. 9" × 12"). Have students cover the cardboard with glued-on pieces of wallpaper scraps (gluing a strip of contrasting paper along the bottom of the cardboard to create a ground line. Encourage the children to add a construction paper window or a door to the collage. Then, have children cut items from the catalog and glue these onto the wallpaper to design a room of their dreams. Have children share their results. How many of them incorporated similar elements into their rooms? Do any of the rooms look *exactly* alike? Why or why not?

## Character Comparison

Provide each child with a copy of the activity sheet on page 113. Ask the children to tell if they think they are a lot like Peter in *Peter's Chair*. Tell the children that this list will help them to see how much they have in common with Peter. When each student has had an opportunity to complete the poll, read each item aloud, and, with a show of hands, count how many children in the class feel the same as Peter. Ask the children to speculate why an author would write about a character who thinks and feels as they do.

# Peter's Chair

| All about Peter: | I am the same as Peter | I am different from Peter |
|---|---|---|
| 1. Peter owns a pet. | ☐ | ☐ |
| 2. Peter sometimes has trouble sharing. | ☐ | ☐ |
| 3. When Peter was mad, he felt like running away. | ☐ | ☐ |
| 4. Peter liked helping. | ☐ | ☐ |
| 5. Peter felt jealous when he thought someone else (his sister) was getting all the attention. | ☐ | ☐ |
| 6. Peter liked looking at his baby picture. | ☐ | ☐ |
| 7. Peter liked fooling his mother. | ☐ | ☐ |

# Tar Beach

by Faith Ringgold
(Crown Publishers, 1991. 28 pp.)

*In 1939, Cassie Louise Lightfoot is an eight-year-old girl who wants to fly wherever she pleases. From her New York City apartment building's rooftop— dubbed "tar beach"—she lets her imagination soar until the stars lift her up and she can fly over the city.* Tar Beach *is the story of endless possibilities and the universal longing for freedom.*

## Before Reading *Tar Beach*

❍ Have children look carefully at the unusual and exquisite illustrations in *Tar Beach*. From looking at the illustrations, ask the children to tell where they believe the story takes place. Have the children suggest whether the story is fact or fiction; have students offer statements to support their reasoning.

## After Reading *Tar Beach*

❍ Ask the children if they believe Cassie *really could* fly over the city. Tell the children that when Cassie says she can "fly," the author is making use of figurative language. Have children look on a map to locate New York City, Harlem and the George Washington Bridge. If possible, show the class photographs of these places. Inform the class that the author is writing about the rooftop of a neighboring apartment building she sees from the roof of her Harlem apartment. (When the author was a child, her family often spent hot summer nights up on the roof—the adults played cards and the children stayed up late, lying on mattresses.)

> FOLLOW-UP ACTIVITIES

## Creative Imagery

Have the students lie on the floor or on mats, and close their eyes. Reread *Tar Beach* and have each of the students imagine that he or she is Cassie flying over the George Washington Bridge. When you are finished, ask the children how it felt to fly. Then, have the children lie down again. Reread page one of *Tar Beach* and then call on the children to imagine what they see as they fly. Tape record this session. Provide paper for the children to illustrate what they looked like while flying, and what they noticed during their flight. Help children transcribe their narrations from the recorder to their illustrations. Bind pages into a book with observations in the order that they occurred in your recording session. Accompany the book's classroom debut with the taped narration.

## Weaving Fact and Fantasy

According to the summary on the *Tar Beach* book jacket, *Tar Beach's* story line "is a seamless weaving of fact, autobiography and African-American history and literature." Help the children to understand the meaning of "autobiography." Then, have the children create picture books depicting a part of their own lives. If they want, the children can mix fiction into their autobiographies by claiming to possess magical abilities as Cassie did. But, if their stories are to resemble the structure of *Tar Beach*, at least part of each autobiography must be true.

## Understanding Discrimination

In *Tar Beach*, Cassie wants to be free and she wants to free her family from their problems, so she daydreams that she is free to fly. On a large chart pad, list the problems Cassie mentions in the book. Help children understand the discrimination African-Americans went through at the time the book takes place. Help them also to understand that just looking or behaving differently is often the basis for such unfair treatment (of African-Americans and others) even today. Following your discussion, offer each student a copy of page 116. After each scenario on the page has been read aloud, have the children jot down possible solutions to each of the situations described. Record each solution on a large chart pad or chalkboard in a column headed by the problem posed. After all of the students' ideas have been recorded, have students notice which solutions suggest changing (rather than accepting) the situation.

Faith Ringgold was born in the Sugar Hill section of Harlem, NY, the setting of *Tar Beach*. She continues to live there today.

# Tar Beach

Kids in your class make fun of the color of your skin. They call you mean names. It feels like no one will be your friend.

Kids in your class make fun of another kid's skin color. You want to be friends with the one they are picking on, but don't want to lose your friends.

In class, your teacher divides you and your classmates into pairs to work on a science project. Your partner doesn't speak English.

You receive a birthday invitation to a party for a classmate. The birthday child is from a different ethnic background from yours. You have never been to her house before.

In class, you are celebrating a classmate's birthday. Another student refuses to eat a cupcake because his religion doesn't believe in celebrating birthdays. Other kids begin to tease him.

# The Quilt Story

By Tony Johnston
(G. P. Putnam's Sons, 1985. 28 pp.)

*In warm poetic text, this book recounts the life of an heirloom quilt. It also tells of two little girls who, though separated by generations, were united in the comfort of the same quilt. It is a different "take" on a similar theme to that of* The Keeping Quilt *and may be read before or after that story. The two stories together might be the basis for a "Quilt" unit.*

## Before Reading *The Quilt Story*

❍ Ask the children if their family (or someone they know) owns something that has been passed down from generation to generation. Remind the children that such an heirloom need not be expensive, but it does need to hold special meaning to the people who keep it. Tell the children that *The Quilt Story* is about such an heirloom. Ask the children to listen carefully to see if they can decide why the heirloom is so special to the characters in the story.

## After Reading *The Quilt Story*

❍ Ask the children to describe the quilts they may have seen. Show the children pictures of different types of popular quilt patterns (featured today even in mail order catalogs). (If the children have already read *The Keeping Quilt*, this may be unnecessary.) Tell the children that quilting is now considered an American folk art, but that the pioneer women who first sewed quilts did so to make the most of fabric scraps (note the old socks sewn into the quilt in *The Quilt Story*), and to bring warmth and color to their sparse, plain homes and rough lives. Ask the children to list all the ways that Abigail used the quilt. How many of the children in class have a favorite blanket or soft toy from their own childhood? Would these possessions make for good heirlooms? Do children of other cultures have favorite toys or possessions? How can the children find out this information?

## FOLLOW-UP ACTIVITIES

## American Folk Toys

Secure a copy of *The Foxfire Book of Toys and Games* (E. P. Dutton, 1985), or any other book featuring a collection of American folk toys and games. Show your class the pictures of the toys which date back more than 200 years to colonial days (and beyond!). Have the class decide how their modern toys are similar to or different from the folk toys (which have no batteries, no electricity, few moving parts and are for the most part homemade). Have the children interview their parents and grandparents to discover what kinds of toys they played with. Did they, too, have a special blanket or toy that they played with for a long time? Were their toys (or blankets or clothes) ever homemade?

## Folk Art Museum

Have children assemble a folk art museum by bringing in to school items reminiscent of colonial times. These may include quilts, toys, jewelry, pictures, tools, gadgets, knick-knacks, etc. (Because of the recent interest in using American folk art for decorating our modern homes, it should not be difficult to gather a collection together.) Label and display the pieces together in a central place for the whole school to enjoy. For more information on quilting, toy making, and colonial times, see *Colonial America (Cooperative Learning Activities)* by Sue Schneck and Mary Strohl (Scholastic, 1991).

## Schoolhouse Quilting Bee

Use quilting books such as *101 Patchwork Patterns* by Ruby McKim (Dover, 1962) to familiarize children with the schoolhouse quilt pattern. Remind children that quilts were often completed by groups of people working together at a social gathering known as a "quilting bee." Each quilter would work on one portion of the quilt, but no individual effort appeared as great as when all the pieces were joined together. Invite each of the children to create one block for a classroom "schoolhouse quilt." Begin by preparing one 9″ × 10″ rectangle of solid colored felt for each student. After cutting felt to size, fold over the top edge of each felt piece to create a 9″ square and to provide a dowel casing (to be used later). You or another adult can then use a hot glue gun to glue casing closed along the long edge, leaving sides open. Provide students with copies of the schoolhouse quilt block pattern on page 119, fabric scraps, and a prepared felt square. Students should first cut apart the pattern pieces on page 119 and then should pin each piece to a different type of fabric (calico, chintz or other fabric scraps available as remnants from fabric stores). After cutting the pattern shapes from the fabric, students should reassemble the design on their felt (being certain to attach the fabric pieces to the front side of the felt opposite the casing attachment). Fabric pieces may be glued on the felt with fabric glue, and/or they may be stitched in place with a running stitch to simulate a quilted look. Felt schoolhouse blocks may be displayed together to create a bulletin board quilt. When you are ready to send the squares home, insert a dowel (12″ long and ⅛″ in diam.) through each casing and tie a length of ribbon to the ends of each dowel to create a wall hanging. (This project may also be completed with construction paper substituting for the felt, and wallpaper scraps substituting for the fabric. Ribbon for hanging may then be taped directly to the back of the paper quilt block.)

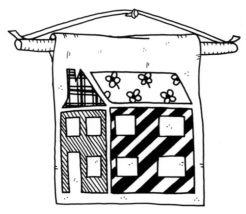

# The Quilt Story

# Matzoh Mouse

by Lauren L. Wohl
(Harper Collins, 1991. 32 pp.)

*Sarah can't wait for the Passover Seder and for all the delicious treats that will follow. Day after day she looks longingly at the boxes of food her mother has stored for the feast. Finally, she can't resist any longer...and once she starts nibbling, she can't stop. What will the grown-ups do if they discover that Sarah is responsible for eating almost all of the chocolate-covered matzoh? Has Sarah ruined the Passover feast?*

## Before Reading *Matzoh Mouse*

❍ Tell the children that this is the story of a girl whose family is preparing for a Jewish holiday named Passover. Ask if any of the children can explain the day to the class. (If none of the children in class celebrates Passover, consider sharing a children's book which explains the holiday such as *Passover* by June Behrens [Children's Press, 1987] and *I Love Passover* by Marilyn Hirsch [Holiday House, 1985]. Christian children familiar with Easter and the Last Supper may be surprised to learn that the Last Supper was a Seder—depending on your class, this can be a wonderful way to get children to think about the interconnectedness of religions, and ultimately, people.) As you read the story to the class, have the children listen for all the ways Sarah helps her family get ready for the special day.

## After Reading *Matzoh Mouse*

❍ Have the children recount how Sarah was helpful in getting ready for the Passover Seder. On a chart pad, list how she was helpful. Have each child in the class recall a special time or holiday they celebrated at home, and how they helped their family prepare. If some children claim they have no jobs at home, have them suggest a job they would like to do next time such a day occurs. How similar were the jobs that the children mentioned compared to the ones Sarah performed?

## FOLLOW-UP ACTIVITIES

### Sample Seder Treats

In *Matzoh Mouse*, Sarah can't wait to taste the Seder sweets: marshmallow treats, jelly slices, macaroons, cashews and chocolate-covered matzoh. Have the children make a list of foods and treats usually associated with other holidays and special times. Provide play clay for the children to mold favorite treats for their friends to pretend to taste. If possible, provide some of the Seder treats mentioned in the book for the class to sample. Also, invite children to take turns hiding and finding a matzoh hidden in a napkin.

### Passover Preparations

Have the children recall what preparations the characters went through to get ready to celebrate Passover. Meet separately with each student. Have students cite a special time they celebrated their lives, then have them talk about the steps they and/or their family take to prepare. Print these special times and preparation steps on individual pieces of paper. Have students take turns pantomiming the preparation and celebration for the rest of the class to guess.

## Sharing A Special Meal

Sharing food together helps bond families. Invite your classroom "family" to brainstorm menu items for a multicultural meal, the ingredients of which can symbolize class unity (and which they can bring from home). A tossed salad of mixed ingredients, for example, can symbolize many different children working together to create a delicious whole.

## Exploring Cultural Symbols

The Jewish seder plate is filled with symbols special to Jewish people and their history. Provide each of the children a copy of page 122 which lists these symbols. Then, have the children locate the same information in *Matzoh Mouse* and have them record the corresponding explanation for each symbol on the activity sheet. Invite the class to think of other cultural or religious holidays and celebrations and related symbols (e.g., Thanksgiving turkeys, Valentine's Day hearts, Hanukkah candles, Christmas stars and angels, etc.). You may choose to show children symbolic objects or pictures of such symbols (usually available in seasonal catalogs and magazines). Then, have the children work together to research and record (on the activity sheet) what these symbols represent. (Research may be as simple or in-depth as the children are able to complete.) Encourage students to share and compare findings.

# Matzoh Mouse

| Symbols | Symbols' Significance (What They Mean) |
|---|---|
| horseradish | |
| parsley | |
| haroseth | |
| matzoh | |
| | |
| | |
| | |
| | |
| | |
| | |

# Katie-Bo: An Adoption Story

by Iris L. Fisher
(Adama Books, 1987. 52 pp.)

*Jim and Teddy's mom is having a baby—but her tummy isn't growing and she doesn't want to eat pickle-and-peanut butter sandwiches. That's because Jim and Teddy's family is adopting a baby. And, because the baby was born in far-away Korea, she will look a bit different from her adoptive brothers. This straightforward account of planning to adopt a foreign-born baby—including visits with a social worker and a few rocky emotional moments—will show readers how such an adoption can be a special way to have a special child join a family.*

## Before Reading *Katie-Bo: An Adoption Story*

❍ Hold a discussion to discover wnat the students already know about adoption. Ask if any of the children want to tell about their own adoption, or about someone they know who is adopted. Help children to imagine if adopting a child from a foreign country might feel different from adopting a child from a similar ethnic or cultural background.

## After Reading *Katie-Bo: An Adoption Story*

❍ Have the children take a close look at the collage technique used to create the pictures in Katie-Bo. Invite them to notice how the artist designed the pictures with a variety of papers and objects including opaque construction paper, maps, wallpaper samples, magazine pictures and tiny plastic toys. Help the children speculate that perhaps the "pieced together" illustrations in the book represent the "coming together" of individual family members—especially in the case of an adoption. As the pieces of a collage are glued together, ask the children to imagine what binds an adoptive child to a family—especially when ethnicity, culture and biology are not common bonds.

> FOLLOW-UP ACTIVITIES

## Create a Class Collage

After your follow-up discussion regarding collages, suggest that the children create their own collage of your classroom family. Begin by having each student create an individual full-length self-portrait collage. Offer the children construction paper, discarded maps, wallpaper samples, magazine pictures, fabric scraps, etc. To assure that the portraits will turn out somewhat uniform in size, offer the children pre-cut rectangles of lightweight oaktag and instruct them to "fill the oaktag with a head-to-toe portrait." Students should lightly sketch their portraits in pencil, taking care to leave lines wide set, simple and "uncluttered." When they are satisfied, students should outline their pictures with black thinline marker. They should then cover the line drawing with a thin sheet of copy paper and trace the drawing onto the paper. Students should then cut apart the closed parts of their drawings and use the pieces as pattern guides for cutting apart materials provided. When materials have been cut, they may be glued to the oaktag line drawing. Students may use paints, markers or yarn to add more color, detail and texture to their collages. When dry, collages may be cut out and attached to the bulletin board to create a huge class collage. If desired, extra paper details representing the classroom furnishings and decor may be added to the display. If possible, photograph the collage and offer each child a copy as a remembrance of their classroom family.

## At Face Value

Provide the class with photographs of famous and ordinary families and individuals cut from magazines. (Parenting and celebrity magazines are a good source for this.) Aim for a selection of pictures representing a variety of ethnic backgrounds. Have the children examine the photographs to discover how the family members and individuals look alike and how they look different. Have each child choose two people—either family members or not—to study and compare. Use copies of page 125 to record this information. Use the exercise to help children understand that members of families bound biologically can be physically different, just as families brought together through adoption can be physically similar. But whether physically similar or different, people have common feelings and experiences that can unite us all in the "family of mankind."

Name _____

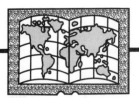

# Katie-Bo: An Adoption Story

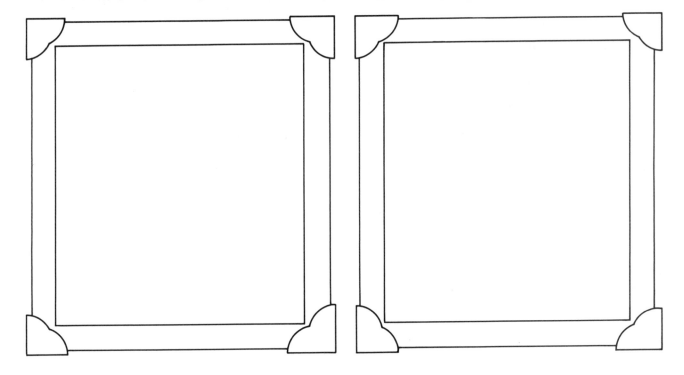

| Eyes | | |
|------|---|---|
| Hair | | |
| Nose | | |
| Age | | |
| Skin Tone | | |
| Height | | |

# Knots on a Counting Rope

by Bill Martin, Jr.
and John Archambault
(Henry Holt, 1987. 32 pp.)

*Under a starry canopy, a Native American grandfather recounts the story of his grandson's birth for the boy (who loves to hear the story again and again). Because the story represents a legacy of courage and strength the boy will need to remember even after the grandfather's death, Grandfather ties one knot on a counting rope with each telling. With his grandfather's love and legacy to carry in his heart, the boy will know the strength he needs to cross the darkest of mountains—his blindness.*

## Before Reading *Knots on a Counting Rope*

○ Ask students to tell if they have ever known or seen anyone who is blind. Ask if the students have ever imagined how it must feel to be blind. Tell the children that this is the story about a boy who is blind from birth. Do the children think the story will be a happy one or a sad one?

## After Reading *Knots on a Counting Rope*

○ Ask the children to tell how Boy-Strength-of-Blue-Horses feels about being blind. Ask: If it is so difficult being blind, why isn't Boy-Strength-of-Blue-Horses sad?

### FOLLOW-UP ACTIVITIES

## Memories

Boy-Strength-of-Blue-Horses loves to listen again and again to his Grandfather's account of the boy's birth and growth. Tell the class that storytelling and a sense of heritage is very important to Native Americans. Use this information to encourage students to record a portion of their own history. Ask children to bring to school a picture of themselves as a young child or as a baby. Then, have children offer oral accounts of something that happened to them when they were younger. Their stories may recount any joyous, funny, sad or scary times they can recall or have been told about, but it is important that the story took place at about the same time as the photo. (e.g., a story of a child's birth would be accompanied by a baby photo, and a story of a child's first day of kindergarten would be accompanied by a photo of the child when he or she was five-years old.) Have the children dictate or write the story they told to the class. Display stories together with the photos on a bulletin board entitled, "His-Stories and Her-Stories."

## Colorful "Feeling" Poems

Boy-Strength-of-Blue-Horses cannot see colors with his eyes, but his grandfather uses elements of nature (e.g., morning, sunrise, lambs' wool, etc.) to help the boy understand the mood of the color blue. Invite students to compose such nature-based poems that might help Boy-Strength-of-Blue-

Horses understand other colors. On a chart pad or chalkboard, print some names of favorite colors. For each color listed, have the children brainstorm physical elements of nature that remind them of that color. Remind children that they must limit elements to those that must be felt or touched to be experienced. (Hint: If this activity proves too difficult for some groups of students, consider having the children close their eyes and imagine what colors various elements of nature *feel* like (e.g., "Sunlight looks yellow. Sunlight *feels* like the color _____ because _____. Leaves look green. Leaves *feel* like the color _____ because _____.). What the thing *feels* like may differ from the color it actually is. For example, sunlight might feel red to some students, because it is hot. Record each student's answers on a large piece of paper.

## Super Strong "Keeping Cards"

*Knots on a Counting Rope* is a story of physical and emotional strength. Ask children to define what it is to be strong. Encourage a broad definition of the term by encouraging input from as many students as possible. Reread those passages from the story that deal directly or indirectly with strength (or print appropriate portions of the text on the blackboard for the class to refer to). Help the children to understand what the passages reveal about the *types of strength* Native Americans value (e.g., strength to overcome physical challenges, strength to face what frightens us, strength of family connection, strength of love, etc.). Use students' familiarity with the above-normal physical strength of Super heroes, professional wrestling stars, and sports figures. Help them reflect on how these characters compare with the characters in *Knots On A Counting Rope*, whose strengths are very different. Use the activity sheet on page 128 to have students create a Super Strong Hero or Heroine "Keeping Card" (similar to the trading cards many children enjoy collecting) whose super strength is *not* like the physical kind of the above mentioned figures, but is more like the kind displayed in *Knots on a Counting Rope*. Have the students draw a picture of their hero or heroine and fill in the blanks at the bottom of the page in the style of their favorite trading cards. Have students paste the completed "keeping cards" on construction paper and display on a "Super Strong Heroes and Heroines" bulletin board.

Name _____

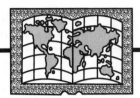

# Knots on a Counting Rope

Create a "Super-Strong Hero or Heroine" with special powers like Boy-Strength-Of-Blue-Horses. Draw a picture of your Hero or Heroine in the space below. Tell about your character on the lines at the bottom.

My hero/heroine's name is: _____.

His/Her special ability is to: _____

_____.

She/He is a heroine/hero because: _____

_____

Her/His greatest adventure happened when: _____

_____.

*Native American*

# The Girl Who Loved Wild Horses

by Paul Gobel
(Bradbury Press, 1978. 32 pp.)

*A Native American girl who loves horses is lost among them during a terrible storm. The leader of the horses then invites the girl to live with them. When, in the end, the girl is one with the horses, it is clear that this lovely story is meant to underscore the Native American people's affinity with and awe of nature.*

## Before Reading *The Girl Who Loved Wild Horses*

❍ Remind the children that Native Americans value having a very close relationship with nature. From the title of the book, can the children guess what aspect of nature this Native American story is about? Ask the class to tell how many of them have ever had the chance to ride a horse or to get close to a horse. What were their reactions to their experiences?

## After Reading *The Girl Who Loved Wild Horses*

❍ Have the class leaf through the book's illustrations to find symbols that they readily associate with Native Americans (e.g., arrows, feathers as hair ornaments, tipis, men with long, braided hair, etc.). What new information did the class learn about Native Americans from reading this book?

FOLLOW-UP ACTIVITIES

## A Natural Mood

Have children raise their hands to indicate how many of them knew (before reading the book) that Native Americans feel close to nature? Ask the children who raised their hands to explain how they learned this information. Invite the class to comb through the book's illustrations to discover how many pictorial references to nature appear in the pages of the book (i.e., look for plants, animals and other natural elements pictured in the book.). List these on a chart pad. Have the children discuss why the author/illustrator would include elements in his pictures that he doesn't directly discuss in the book.

## Labeling People

It is possible that some students in class will refer to Native Americans as "Indians." Tell the class that such labels are often a controversial topic even among the people belonging to the culture. Print the two labels on a blackboard. Ask the class to tell what they know about each label. If possible, invite a Native American person to visit your class to discuss the origin of each label and importance of being sensitive to such labels.

## Native American Symbols

Draw attention to the symbols featured on the Native American tipis. As much as the students are able to interpret the symbols shown, have them describe which symbols feature elements of nature (e.g., the sun, horses, deer, fish, etc.). Consider sharing the book *Painted Tipis* by Contemporary Plains Indian Artists in cooperation with the Indian Arts and Crafts Board of the U.S. Department of the Interior (Oklahoma Indian Arts and Crafts Cooperative, 1973). Provide students with copies of the activity on page 131 which features additional Native American symbols. Provide each student with a paper tipi. To construct tipis, trace around a dinner plate which has been placed on brown craft paper. Use a marker to place a dot in the center of each circle, and cut a straight line from the edge of the circle to the dot. Provide students with markers, and encourage students to use the markers to decorate their tipis with the symbols provided. When tipis are decorated, staple to form cone shapes and staple to a bulletin board to create a native American village. Have students use paint and markers to add background details, animals and people to the scene. Ask the children to tell if they believe that all Native Americans live or lived in tipis. (For more information and activities about Native Americans, see *Native Americans Cooperative Learning Activities* by Susan Schneck and Mary Strohl, (Scholastic, 1991).

Name _____

# The Girl Who Loved Wild Horses

canoe

camp

hear

night

rain

buffalo head

fish

buffalo hoof

bravest

bear paw

snake

horse

lightning

stars

otter

mountain

# Russian-American

# The Keeping Quilt
by Patricia Polacco
(Simon and Schuster, 1988. 32 pp.)

*This book recounts the story of an heirloom quilt, crafted from a basket of old clothes including Uncle Vladimir's shirt, Aunt Havalah's nightdress, and an apron of Aunt Natasha's. Once completed, the quilt is passed down through four generations in a family. For nearly a century, the quilt serves such purposes as a Sabbath tablecloth, a wedding canopy and a baby receiving blanket. The quilt is also a constant reminder of—and tribute to—family loved ones back home in Russia.*

## Before Reading *The Keeping Quilt*

❍ Review these terms with the class: generation, heirloom, inheritance, legacy. Then, have the children describe any items that have been passed down from generation to generation in their families, such as houses, furniture, dishes, artwork, toys, etc. Remind the children that such legacies needn't be items worth a lot of money. Items such as photographs, knick-knacks, clothing and toys may also be handed down from generation to generation—and may be worth more to the receiver than any sum of money! Tell the children that *The Keeping Quilt* is a story of just such a legacy.

## After Reading *The Keeping Quilt*

❍ Invite students to take a close look at the artwork in the book. What do they notice about the use of color? Have the class make a list of possible reasons why the author/illustrator chose to use color so carefully? Ask: How would the book appear different if each of the illustrations was in full color? Why is the quilt so valuable to the author/illustrator? Would the quilt be as valuable to us? Why or why not?

## FOLLOW-UP ACTIVITIES

## Make a Class Quilt

Following are directions for creating a class quilt. If you complete the project early enough in the school year, each student may have a chance to be the keeper of the quilt for a few days or a week. After that, the quilt can become a legacy that the class leaves behind for the classroom or school—or the quilt may be donated to a hospital, nursing home, homeless shelter or day care center.

To begin, provide each child with two plain pieces of copy paper (each trimmed to 8½″ square) and fabric crayons (available in craft stores). Instruct each child to use the crayons and one piece of paper to draw something they care about or value in their lives (e.g., a toy, a book, a pet, something in nature, etc.). On the other piece of paper, have children trace one of their hands and color it in. You or another adult can then use an iron to transfer the drawing onto individual squares of fabric (approximately 10″ square) or onto a white or pastel solid-colored flat sheet. (Directions on the

crayon box will guide your fabric and sheet selection.) The dimensions of the quilt will depend on the number of students in the class—a class of 24 students will produce 48 squares—enough squares for a quilt of 6 squares wide by 8 squares long. Using handprint squares as a border, pin individual squares of decorated fabric right sides together to create strips.
Stitch on a sewing machine, then join the strips together
to create a quilt top. Pin the top of the quilt to a batting backing (available in craft and fabric stores), and show the children how to stitch around their fabric designs, thus creating a quilted effect. When completed, cover the quilt top with a second sheet or fabric piece trimmed to fit the quilt top. Use a machine to stitch three sides of the quilt shut, creating a "pillow case" effect. Turn the quilt right side out, tuck the raw ends inside, and, finally, stitch the fourth side closed.

## Legacies and Inheritances

Have students think about what they would like to hand down to someone they love. Have students also think about the gifts they have inherited from their ancestors. Remind children that an inheritance need not be something expensive or even something you can touch. Rather, it can also be a lesson learned from someone loved, a way of being, or a special time spent together. Use copies of the story frame on page 134 to have children first draw what they have inherited or what they might hand down, and then write a brief description of why the legacy or inheritance is so important to them. If children are tempted to write abbreviated descriptions (e.g., "I like the book Aunt Sara gave me because it's nice."), encourage students to use sensory imagery ("it feels like, it looks like, it smells like, etc.") to tell specifically *why* the gift was nice and what it reminds them of.

## Learning Legacy

Traditionally, many graduating classes write a "Last Will and Testament" that then appears in their yearbook or school paper. Although this tradition is usually something of a lampoon of things and people in the school, you can adapt it to help your students understand legacies and inheritances better. Invite students to brainstorm the best experiences they had as a class this year, what they learned, etc., and write them on a "scroll" to be passed on as a legacy to the next year's class.

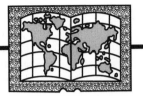

# The Keeping Quilt

_____

_____

_____

_____

_____

_____

_____

_____

_____

# Angel Child, Dragon Child

by Michele Maria Surat
(Carnival Press, 1983. 35 pp.)

*This is the tender story of Ut, a young Vietnamese girl who must adjust to her new American school without the help of her mother (who could not afford yet to leave Vietnam). How Ut finally becomes friends with her new classmates, and how these same children help reunite Ut with her mother, make for an endearing story of human courage and love.*

## Before Reading *Angel Child, Dragon Child*

❍ Have children examine the soft, muted colors artist Vo-Dinh Mai uses to illustrate the cover and text of the book. Explain to children that an artist's techniques and preferences can be influenced by the culture in which he or she grew up. Visit the library to observe works by other Vietnamese artists. Are the children able to find works that look similar to the book's illustrations?

## After Reading *Angel Child, Dragon Child*

❍ Ut knows she looks different from the American children, and she knows they look different from her. What does Ut notice about the American children that is different (e.g., their long noses, their round eyes, etc.)? What do they notice about her (e.g., her clothing, her language, etc.)? Why do the American children tease Ut about the way she dresses? Why doesn't she tease them back? Ask the class to talk about how Ut felt on her first day in the American school. Describe how she might feel different if she were attending school in Vietnam.

> ### FOLLOW-UP ACTIVITIES

## Pastel Water Colors

After observing the illustrations in *Angel Child, Dragon Child*, suggest that the children may approximate the art featured in the book by painting with pastel water colors. For their paintings, you may either provide children with paint boxes or purchase tubes of real water colors from art stores. Also, look to art books for inspiration and try approximating other kinds of artwork from Vietnam. Display finished pieces together with the title: "Vietnam-Inspired Art."

## Matchbox Photo Keepers

Encourage children to share family photo albums with the class. Have children brainstorm a list of reasons why people keep such pictures. Talk about the importance of Ut's matchbox photo of her mother. Ask the children if they ever wished they could talk to their mother (or another family member or friend) when they were not near. Invite the children to make their own matchbox photo keeper. Ask children to bring in a small photo of someone they love. (It must be a photo each child can keep.)

Provide children with empty matchboxes. Help children to trim their pictures to fit inside matchboxes by placing matchboxes on top of photos, tracing around matchboxes and cutting along lines with scissors. Open the matchboxes and spread the floor of each with white glue. Ease each photo into place in a box; let dry. Allow children to keep their matchbox keepers in school, so they may "visit" with their loved ones whenever they wish.

## Sorting Out Feelings

Have children research to discover the significance of dragons in Asian cultures. (Unlike the fire-breathing dragons of Europe, cloud-breathing dragons of Asian mythology were usually well-meaning creatures prone to fits of rage. This may explain why, when angry, Ut labels herself a "Dragon Child.") Provide children with copies of page 137. Have them review *Angel Child, Dragon Child* to discover which of Ut's feelings and actions belong to the "Angel Child" and which belong to the "Dragon Child." Jot these in the space provided on the activity sheet. Brainstorm to create a list of feelings which would be difficult to categorize by the simple angel/dragon criteria (e.g., sadness, confusion, fear, loneliness, etc.). Challenge the children to create new categories for these feelings; record both the categories and the feelings on the activity sheet. Review the list to see how many of the children have experienced the feelings listed, thus helping the children to understand that such feelings are something we share in common.

Vo-Dinh Mai, illustrator of *Angel Child, Dragon Child* was born in Hue, Vietnam.

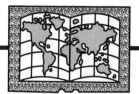

# Angel Child, Dragon Child

| "Angel Child" Feelings | "Dragon Child" Feelings |
| --- | --- |
| | |

# List of Publishers

Adama Books
Imprint of Franklin K. Watts, Inc.
387 Park Ave. South
New York, NY 10016

Atheneum
866 Third Ave.
New York, NY 10022

Bradbury Press
866 Third Ave
New York, NY 10022

Carolrhoda Books, Inc.
241 First Ave. North
Minneapolis, MN 55401

Children's Book Press
1416 Ninth Ave.
San Fransisco, CA 94122

Children's Press
1224 West Van Buren St.
Chicago, IL 60607

Cobblehill
c/o Penguin, U.S.A
Box 120
Bergenfield, NJ 07621

Coward, McCann and Geohegan
Imprint of Putnam
200 Madison Ave.
New York, NY 10016

Crown Publishers
225 Park Ave. South
New York, NY 10003

Dial Books for Young Readers
375 Hudson St.
New York, NY 10014

Doubleday & Co.
666 Fifth Ave.
New York, NY 10103

E.P. Dutton
2 Park Ave.
New York, NY 10016

Dutton Children's Books
357 Hudson St.
New York, NY 10016

Harcourt Brace Jovanovich
1250 Sixth Ave.
San Diego, CA 92101

HarperCollins
(formerly Harper and Row)
10 E. 53 St.
New York, NY 10022

Henry Holt and Co.
521 Fifth Ave.
New York, NY 10175

Holt, Rinehart and Winston
383 Madison Ave.
New York, NY 10017

Alfred A. Knopf
201 E. 50 St.
New York, NY 10022

J.B. Lippencott Junior Books
10 East 53 St.
New York, NY 10022

Little, Brown & Co.
34 Beacon St.
Boston, MA 02108

Lothrop, Lee and Shepard Books
105 Madison Ave.
New York, NY 10016

Macmillan
866 Third Ave.
New York, NY 10022

Philomel Books
200 Madison Ave.
New York, NY 10016

Scholastic, Inc.
730 Broadway
New York, NY 10003

Simon and Schuster Books for Young Readers
1230 Avenue of the Americas
New York, NY 10020

Thomas Y. Crowell, Jr. Books
10 E. 53 St.
New York, NY 10022

Viking Press
375 Hudson St.
New York, NY 10014

G.P. Putnam's Sons
51 Madison Ave.
New York, NY 10010

Frederick Warne & Co.
27 Wrights Lane
London W85T2
England

Albert Whitman
6340 Oakton St.
Morton Grove, IL 60053

# Notes

# Notes

Notes

# Notes

# Notes

# Notes